BECOMING a
HOLISTIC ENTREPRENEUR

Advance Praise

"I absolutely love how this book is organized! The spiritual aspect is tied to the practical steps and that's what makes *Becoming a Holistic Entrepreneur* so magical!"

—**Kim Adams**, Owner & Web Designer with
KokuaMediaSolutions.com

"I got chills and deeply resonated with reading this, especially the exercise Remembering Your Sacred Why! to alleviate burnout. So grateful! I also love the physical exercise example for sustaining energy. Both of those are so important to keep one going through the doubts and exhaustion of trying to be in this business."

— **Tricia Marsh**, Founder & Holistic Nutrition Coach,
Mandalamountainhealth.com

"Candid and encouraging, this book provides clarity in your step-by-step process addressing the emotional, mental, physical and spiritual growth path within New Opportunity. This is an inspired energy work and will be a motivational, incremental guide to help one engage in growth, learning, and new purpose."

— **Steve James**, Principal Architect, DTJ Design

"From the moment I started reading, I felt like Grace was seeing me deeply and speaking directly to my heart. Grace brings an immediate sense of safety and support. She provides a golden path to follow and the clear instructions I have always wished for. The way to get from here to the prize is successful sacred service, fully living my authentic life. With Grace by my side, I know I can do this."

— **Isa Maria**, Professional Fine Artist and
Non-Violent Communications Facilitator

"I love the feeling this builds to add (ad)venture to the Dream Holistic Healing Business startup. Grace's writing is spirited, uplifting, and delicious amidst it's supporting, enlightening, and expertly guided steps. The Elevator-Up process will take you there!"

— **Pamela Schrack**, Owner, Aloha Consulting

BECOMING a
HOLISTIC
ENTREPRENEUR

*7 Steps to Your
Sustainable Success*

Grace Danielle Meek

NEW YORK

LONDON • NASHVILLE • MELBOURNE • VANCOUVER

BECOMING a HOLISTIC ENTREPRENEUR
7 Steps to Your Sustainable Success

Published in New York, New York, by Morgan James Publishing in partnership with Difference Press. Morgan James is a trademark of Morgan James, LLC. www.MorganJamesPublishing.com

ISBN 978-1-64279-999-6 paperback
ISBN 978-1-63195-000-1 eBook
ISBN 978-1-63195-001-8 audio
Library of Congress Control Number: 2020900876

Cover Design:
Rachel Lopez

Editor:
Emily Tuttle

Book Coaching:
The Author Incubator

Morgan James is a proud partner of Habitat for Humanity Peninsula and Greater Williamsburg. Partners in building since 2006.

Get involved today! Visit
www.MorganJamesBuilds.com

This Elevator–Up! is dedicated to the Inviting Balance Tribe.
Thank you for trust, our times, and this cocreation.
Thank you for inspiring me to Journey the Length of the Light.

TABLE OF CONTENTS

Chapter 1

NOW IS YOUR TIME TO START YOUR DREAM HOLISTIC HEALING BUSINESS

"Do not wait: the time will never be 'just right'. Start where you stand, and work whatever tools you may have at your command and better tools will be found as you go along."

– Napoleon Hill

Are you repeatedly noticing that conventional work environments aren't designed to leverage all the holistic knowledge, healing gifts, and learning journeys you deeply desire to express and explore? It's likely that you're experiencing increasing impatience and irritability at work, and it's nudging you to consider what is next for you professionally. Is staying comfortable at your day job less attractive with each payday? Maybe you have become numb to the creative impulses that initially made you such a refreshing asset at work. Does the time and energy you are contributing to your job leave you exhausted and wondering if what you are doing is really making a positive, holistic impact in your world? You have probably found yourself adrift in thoughts about how there must be something more meaningful you are meant to contribute to the world. These are all signs that the time to start your dream Holistic Healing Business is *now!*

Every healer has a spark within them that illuminates the question, "How do I live my full potential *and* joy through service to others?" Some find satisfying service alignments through conscious parenting, caring for a beloved elder, or working for their favorite non-profit or spiritual organization. But others, like yourself, find themselves curious and inspired to share the unique purpose of their particular holistic perspectives in support of the greater good of all. Maybe feedback from your friends, family, community, or Spirit is telling you that your support *elevates* them and is valued beyond just being a good person and global citizen. If your healing experiences inspire more curiosity than judgement and it makes you smile from your center to help others allow healing into their lives, you are ready to shift toward a life of deeply gratifying service as a Holistic Healer.

This seven-level Elevator–Up! process will guide you from figuring out the optimal way to transition from your current work to having all that you need to launch your *dream* Holistic Healing Business (HHB.) If you manifested this process at a time when you *just* decided to start your HHB, *trust* how powerfully the clarity of that decision is aligning you now with everything you need to enjoy this exciting, new professional and personal development adventure. You will be expertly guided on exactly how to make the most of the time, money, skills, and other reSources you already have. You don't have to be stuck another moment in the fear and frustration emerging healers often feel when they get to the point that making this leap of faith is less risky and painful than staying stuck. Following this seven level process, you will benefit from the experiences of many holistic entrepreneurs that have done this upleveling work already and who now serve and thrive in the gratitude that comes from knowing that they are living in alignment with their Healing Gifts and Higher Purpose. Many holistic healers who I have personally helped start their HHBs previously spent decades and fortunes to discover principles that this process quickly captures and puts in practical terms for you. They now report significant, relevant expansion of both their Healing Gifts and their capacities to deliver them. Here's what they felt they gained from the process:

- Improved sense of safety, clarity, and self-confidence with their Healing Gifts
- Focused understanding of what they want and how they want it within their HHB
- Increased commitment to their most efficient and effective HHB decisions
- Connected sense of belonging and service to the community around their HHB

- Simplified truthfulness and communication about their Healing Gifts and their HHB
- Expanded financial and resource abundance from improving their sensory skills
- Secured HHB longevity through cocreating sustainable value with their clients and community

When Is the Best Time to Uplevel?

For some healers, an incident or situation creates a clear break in their ability to stay in their current work *and* keep their integrity. For others, a physical healing crisis finds a remedy in a previously unexplored holistic healing method that ignites the HHB service spark within them. Others make the shift to find a healthier outlet for their creativity that previously manifested in addiction, distraction, and/or depression when they suppressed or ignored their Gifts. Still others are fortunate enough to embrace alignment with their healer's heart, as it is passed down through many generations within their family or tribe.

For example, several of the female bodyworkers and one of the male energy workers I have worked with discovered or deepened relationships with biological relatives who they learned have similar Gifts through the first level work of this process. This very healing outcome debunks the myth that embracing your Healing Gifts will likely lead to your exile from existing family, friends, and community. Whatever path has led you to your sacred service alignment, know that this upleveling process empowers you to become your best self on your terms and at your own pace. Many proven and refined entrepreneurial techniques herein support you becoming a

Healing Elevator of others, in alignment with the Highest Good of All.

The first aspect this Elevator–Up! process will guide you through is *feeling* and *knowing* you have enough time, money, reSources, and skills to succeed at starting your dream Holistic Healing Business from where you're at *now*. You will be guided through figuring out how to trust yourself and this process so that all your planning, investments, perceived risks, and rewards can be navigated from a position of thriving versus a survival mentality.

You will transcend your fears about leaving your current work by creating your peaceful, powerful, positive job exit, which will free up massive amounts of entrepreneurial energy for your dream HHB beginning. This precious creative energy is often overlooked and is vital to organizing and implementing the countless ideas that have been clamoring around in your dreams and waking fantasies about how to make a difference in the world. Upleveling your professional potential as a holistic healer, all while getting and staying grounded in a reality you are both comfortable with and inspired by, is a *core principle* of this process. It ensures that the emotional, physical, mental, and spiritual aspects of your being are *holistically* harmonized as you uplevel your unique and priceless Healing Gifts.

This Elevator–Up! process also gently helps you see the high cost of staying stuck/unclear. What are you getting out of not moving forward in service with your invaluable Healing Gifts? The soul-eroding growth blocks that have been in your spiritual blind spots will be illuminated in direct and empowering ways so that you can decide when, if, and how you are ready to evolve.

Let's face it; if you wanted to be bullied into unsustainable business success, you probably wouldn't be chomping at the bit to leave your mainstream job for something more humane, uplifting, and in greater alignment with your wise holistic healer within.

Honoring Your Growth and Timing as You Uplevel through This Process

Creating your optimal transition plan into your Holistic Healing Business simply, smartly, and safely is accomplished progressively over the course of seven levels. The levels can realistically be transcended in as quickly as eight weeks with the right level of commitment, personal focus, and the aligned guidance of an expert coach. You will know and *feel* as we ascend the levels if you need to take more time in any particular level. This process can be adapted to accommodate whatever comes alive in you and your life situation while you progress. You will also create a customized Holistic Healing Business Starting Plan in this process. This plan is designed to provide a balance of flexibility and structure that evolves as you practice thinking in and outside of the box of typical business startup methods.

By embracing this customizable Elevator–Up! process for amplifying your Healing Gifts, service desires, and holistic career goals, you give yourself and your clients the gift of clarity and safety in all that you facilitate for them as a healer. Issues that show up when healers begin their entrepreneurial efforts without a clear, grounded plan are easily avoidable. As you learn to implement your best practices that these levels help you discover within yourself, you will increasingly be able to authentically guide others in understanding and using their own inner compasses.

As you move through the warm-up exercises, HHB business plan building assignments, and stories about how other healers are thriving by following their hearts and intuition *with a flexible plan,* you will start to see that this accelerated process to becoming a Holistic Entrepreneur is very doable by *you, now!* We focus on leveraging all the conscious effort and unconscious inner compass skills you have already been walking your path with for many years. Also, when "mistakes" do arise, this process has safeguards for ensuring that you gain the best potential lessons and the awareness to choose better for yourself and your clients moving forward.

Effectively starting your Holistic Healing Business *will* lift and evolve all aspects of your life experience in countless ways that may be beyond your current imagining. Together in this seven-level process, we will safely look at the full spectrum of potential faith leaps to understand exactly where you are starting from. Whether you are at "I know exactly what I want from my HHB, but I just want to make sure I don't hurt myself or my clients," or you're all the way over at, "Yikes!, I've just smacked the healing hive; what do I do next?" you will gain invaluable insights about how your emotional, physical, mental, and spiritual realities will be impacted and expanded within the safe structure of this process. You will enjoy expert guidance on how to best take advantage of all the opportunities you may not even recognize as you navigate this most sacred growth curve.

Spoiler Alert: The biggest secret you will uncover as you are elevated by forces seen and unseen through this process is that the hardest part was getting to where you now stand. Right here, right now—with your heart and your hands ready to embrace a better life full of meaning and adventure. Let's get this party started.

Elevator–Up!

Chapter 2
ALIGNING EXPERIENCED, HOLISTIC BUSINESS STARTING HELP

As I say Yes to life, life says Yes to me!
– Louise Hay

As the evening sunlight slants sideways into Metamorphose Yoga studio on Kaua'i, Hawai'i, I am overwhelmed with gratitude for the holistic life I have had the courage to cocreate with Source and many other holistic healers. My restorative yoga class is settling into the sound of my voice and a crystal healing bowl melding together for a delish fifteen-minute savasana. Never in a million years could I have imagined how full my everyday life as a Holistic Healer would become with soul-satisfying moments like this.

Rewinding twenty years, I was at a very common yet sacred crossroads that I have come to understand almost every healer must navigate. It was 8:30 PM, and I was waiting for a flight home at a West Virginia airport. I was intensely checking messages and making logistical arrangements for a tech client's trade show that would yield another sixty-five-plus-hour, *meaningless* work week. So, I guzzled down another venti something to stay ahead of the ball.

Did I have creative freedom as VP of Business Development with a boutique metro DC marketing firm? Absolutely. I had all the freedom in the world to watch my most fertile years and energies get story-boarded, designed, produced, and set-up for the big industry event—and then tossed in the dumpster as my client sold out to a Silicon Valley behemoth, disappearing into the high-tech sunset with what amounted to hush money. As this pattern repeated time and again, the thrill of chasing my six-figure income began to lose its luster, and my health started to show signs that this was an unsustainable cycle. As my appetite, sleep and libido continued to wane, I couldn't seem to muster the energy or clarity to escape this downward spiral.

At a holiday gathering, my aunt gently suggested I connect with a healing intensive she had just completed called The Hoffman Quadrinity Process. She said it would help me find some peace and balance around the challenges I had been overachieving my way away from for as long as I could remember. It was December, and the overwhelming depression that emerged in me every winter was looming large as the sideways sleet froze solid to my windshield. *Enough,* I thought. There has got to be something more to make of my life than enduring this misery for a two-week vacation I would never be able to enjoy knowing the email and paperwork blizzard that would be awaiting my return. When old friends tried to squeeze into my overbooked schedule for lunch, I would more often than not decline, eat Taco Bell in my car, then swish my "car mouthwash" in the parking lot before my next two or four client meetings. And then destiny intervened. A year after my aunt's suggestion and twelve hours before the deadline for the next Quadrinity process, I was surprised to see that a delinquent corporate client had sent in their final payment that yielded a commission that equaled the *exact* amount it cost would cost me to attend the Fall 1999 Quadrinity process. God-bumps, everywhere... So, off I went to fix myself so that I could better tolerate my career choices and get a handle on my flagging marriage. Surely if my husband and I had survived law school, I could pull myself together with a little R&R and goal-rebooting...

Eleven days later, pants on fire and palms recovering from the multiple three-hour stretches of cathartic pounding release work, I returned home forever changed by the mystical healing power of personal development work done in the safety and solidarity of a cohort. Within thirty days, I had amicably resigned from my job (I had developed a sudden, acute allergy to office politics), started a microscopic holistic consulting business, sheepishly asked my college sweetheart if he would either agree to start a family *now* or get divorced, and started Massage Therapy school. I remember thinking how cool it would be to get paid for helping people relax... and that I could nap on my table between clients. No plan; just a shear vertical drop into all my unresolved issues while figuring out how to pay my $3,500 per month in living expenses.

Benefiting from My Decades of HHB Trials and Errors

Over the last two decades, I have experimented with a wide variety of HHB scenarios, including servicing clients from my home office, working as a mobile provider near my home, maintaining a solo healing practice location, collaborating in groups of other healers and/or HHBs, and working online remotely, as I have been on my own Healing Walkabouts. Along the way, I have embraced and leveraged the impact of my work and personal relationships evolving, making some financial decisions from fear, the hidden costs of indecision and distractions, learning to give and receive in balance, communicating my truths and sacred No Thank Yous, sensing who to trust with what and when, and discovering why I am *really* here.

As the last paragraph triggers self-awareness for you about some of the concerns that may be holding you back from starting *your* HHB now, know that the only insurmountable mistake you can make has already been transcended because you are still reading. Congratulations. By continuing to show up here, you have already *energetically* started your HHB, which is the only thing related to your HHB that you alone can do. You can think of this beginning moment like first time you fell in love for real. You may not yet fully understand how your HHB will grow you, but you can feel in your body-mind-spirit that you are now more alive, awake, and connected to your life than ever before.

Would I change anything about starting my own HHB? *Yes,* I would and did change most of it several times over the following three years until I finally hit my stride enough to support myself financially and reSourcefully with just my HHB. I thoroughly enjoyed that plateau for several years. Even though I began my journey in 1999 as an aspiring Certified Massage Therapist, my ideal clients would only take yes for an answer in 2006 when I cautiously began offering intuitive readings. By 2007, I started Clarion Sphere Intuitive Gatherings to be in community around my Healing Gifts. In 2010 my HHB, which I call Inviting Balance, was balanced enough for me to receive the massive Downlove that became the Intuitive Expansion Training Series. It was through helping others remember and develop their own Healing Gifts that I found and polished my HHB genius. Lucky for you, I took copious physical, emotional, mental, and spiritual notes included herein to ensure that if you decide to make your own HHB mistakes just for the fun of it, then at least you will know how to reverse engineer a feasible escape hatch.

This Elevator–Up! Holistic Healing Business starting process evolved to its current bionic strength through a ten-year journey of examining what processes and principles have created measurable success for a wide variety of healing service providers. Some of the initial processes focused primarily on harnessing the Law of Attraction. Then clients started recommitting to further work with the intention of expanding their own intuitive healing skills into their work, ranging from Conscious Architect to Earth Advocate to Holistic Artist to Fulltime Love Mom. I knew then that helping people develop their own HHBs was the next step for my Holistic Healing Business.

Many times over the last decade, I have been asked when I was going to write a DIY manual for healers to wrangle their business thingys and whatevers. So, I tuned in intuitively and asked Source how I could most effectively quantify the best practices and knowledge for developing an HHB for my existing clients, as well as new holistic business builders. It became clear that it was time to write this book to document and streamline this Elevator-UP! process. I knew it could be done simply, safely, and smartly in as little as eight weeks, which is how long it took for this book to go from a potential service refining tool to the magical, sacred service carpet ride I am beyond proud and grateful to share with you!

Fortunately for us both, I had way more courage than common sense at the beginning, and I can look back now on a rich landscape of brave "holistic business feasibility studies" with great satisfaction. This streamlined Elevator–Up! process ensures that countless others will benefit from my lessons learned. So, whether you're wondering what learning and teaching yoga while cruising around the Western US in an RV on your own with a massage table is like or how to relocate with a partner from a liberal coast to the conservative middle for your partner's job all while starting your healing business anew, then I've got the spiritual schwag for you!

Over the past two decades, I have gathered priceless intel about many ways you can learn and thrive professionally by channeling your healing talents into a successful Holistic Healing Business. I have lived and thrived by offering therapeutic massage and aromatherapy in a spare room of my home and in a spare room at a friend's mainstream business while I focused on incorporating optimal anti-aging products that added profound value to my client services. I have traveled extensively while serving individuals and groups of Soul Heroes with my Intuitive Expansion Trainings in places so beautiful, they take your breath away.

Ultimately, I settled into my dream life with my beloved Raymond on the Garden Island of Kauai, Hawai'i, where I awake every day to a symphonic soundscape we call 'birdrise' just before dawn. I sketch this journey to illustrate that until you get started, your dream life will remain a two-dimensional fantasy in someone else's Facebook feed. All that your HHB will become depends first and foremost on if, when, and how you begin. As Oprah says, "Here's what I know for sure." If *I*, of average intelligence and reSources, can figure out how to cocreate a life beyond my wildest dreams, *you* can definitely leverage my cliff (jumping) notes to create your dream Holistic Healing Business, sans most of the chaos and stress!

Chapter 3

THE ELEVATOR–UP! HHB STARTING PROCESS OVERVIEW AND RESULTS

This chapter will overview how this Elevator–Up! seven-level process will help you joyfully embrace and sustainably start sharing your Healing Gifts through your successful Holistic Healing Business *now*.

This process is structured to help you transcend seven main levels of concerns, questions, and inspirations many Holistic Healers go through while starting their dream HHBs. If you already work with the seven basic chakras, you will enjoy how each of the levels addresses issues that may arise around the related chakra. As you ascend to the seventh level, you will have the opportunity to holistically explore how your relationship to each of these energy centers may be enhancing or challenging your new HHB initiatives.

For example, starting at the "root"/first chakra in Level One, we get to the root of your business-starting fears, family issues, trust questions, etc. This allows you to ascend to the second level that deals with *wants*, feeling and knowing that your basic *needs* were addressed first. This is the simplest way I know to build trust in yourself and this process to meet your HHB starting needs. Another major benefit of this method is that it frees up lots of stuck energies and/or resistance. Throughout your upleveling, this energy can be repurposed to fuel your creativity, intuition and right actions for making your dream HHB a reality with more ease.

Learning Styles; Are You a Sprint Horse or a Pack Mule?

Each level provides a warm-up that you can choose to playfully *or* intensely approach, depending upon what your authentic mood is at the beginning of that level. If you're feeling neutral at the start of a new level, then taking it lightly may even be *fun* for you. When you are feeling positively or negatively charged, an intense approach to the level warm-ups can help you intuitively rebalance and support yourself, keeping an open heart and beginner's mind for that level's work.

If it is important to you to have a written business plan that aligns with your holistic values, then you will want to complete the holistic business plan building assignments at the end of each of the seven level chapters. They will help you break down the task of creating your HHB business plan into smaller, simpler tasks that track with the level you are working through. If you are unclear about the value of *at least* drafting a business plan outline, ask yourself,

"Would an outsider understand and/or invest time, money, resources and reputation in my HHB as without a clear, written plan?"

If you prefer to binge read this book first and then work through the levels at your convenience, then I will simply ask you, "Do you want to Supersize that?" If so, have a highlighter and post-its handy to mark areas that have more relevance to your particular business's beginning, learning curves, and interests. This book makes a great "how-to" inspiration manual you can stash in your healing space for when you are waiting between clients or feel inspired by something that came up in a session that has you thinking about an aspect of your HHB development.

Working each level for *at least* a week will yield you an HHB launch in about eight weeks. This way also gives your brain and nervous system a sense of following a trusty map, so they can ease up on your spirit a little with all the should's, supposed-to's, and random panic button-pushing. Just tune in to which way would best float your boat right now while you are still full of the hope you feel having made the decision to exit your day job!

Disclaimer: Be sure to give your inner critic/perfectionist the heads up that they have been downsized via your decision to be elevated out of your current work. They can report to the Department of Unlimited Do-overs on Level Three if they are willing to receive the occupational therapy available to them to retool their perspectives and work off some of the emotional exhaustion they have been charging against the credit *you* deserve for moving forward!

Elevator–Up! Process Overview

On Level One: *Trust* (Root Chakra), you *secure* the clarity and confidence you need to start your dream Holistic Healing Business from exactly where you are *now*. By addressing what fears you are facing about leaving your job, such as running out of money, negative onlookers, and your own conscious and unconscious self-doubts, we create a grounded foundation for your confidence to take root and flourish. Every time you encounter a mental speedbump or emotional downpour, you will be able to simply come back to this very practical beginning level and make progressive adjustments that match what you have already clarified about your values, dreams, desires, and blind spots when you started level one.

On Level Two: *Satisfaction* (Sacral Chakra), you repurpose all the energy freed up on Level One by focusing on your authentic desires to *cocreate* satisfying healing results for both your HHB clients and you. When your holistic healing [ad] venture is designed well enough to take care of you as well as your clients, you will experience the joy of expressing your creativity from a place of thriving versus surviving within your new business. Getting clear on your truest desires for your work life and gradually accepting more self-permission to live them gives your clients permission to do the same in their journeys. Mastering this aspect creates priceless value in your relationships with clients. Also, we work through how to handle the fact that desires are a moving target that ignite and burn-out over and over again as you uplevel. You can see this truth in your current work life. Are your desires the same at work now as they were when you started there?

On Level Three: *Direction* (Solar Plexus Chakra), you develop the *willpower* to make effective and sustainable decisions and adjustments to direct your Holistic Healing Business actions as you grow. Because you have addressed your needs at Level One and focused your desires for your HHB at Level Two, you have upleveled your perspective enough to be more capable at figuring out and sticking to the direction your lower levels have clarified and aligned. You will be learning how to deal with conflicting impulses, such as the temptation to compare and compete and your ego's good and challenging defense mechanisms like perfectionism, self-sabotage, numbing out, confusion, distractions, and criticism.

On Level Four: *Connection* (Heart Chakra), you start embracing and enjoying heart-centered *connecting* that magnetizes clients to your Holistic Healing Business. At this level, you begin to expand your emphasis from *me* to *we*. With many of the aspects of being a confident, integrous healer covered on the first three levels, you can now start to open up to *how much* and *which kinds* of cooperation feel empowering for your HHB. Becoming aware of how your role as a healer impacts your community on many levels helps you minimize drama and keep interpersonal challenges from breaking the heart of your business. Here, you will begin to understand how your capacity for caring uplifts your clients *and* everyone they care about vicariously through the power of the unconditionally loving Source that carries your healing home.

On Level Five: *Ease* (Throat Chakra), you practice communicating authentically and consistently to strengthen your Holistic Healing Business message. If you have ever been grossed out by what you perceive as a "phony" healer, guru, politician, or leader, then you already understand the value of this level for helping create communication ease in your new HHB for clients and yourself. We will try on lots of different healer messaging techniques and templates so you can feel comfortable powerfully communicating who you are and how you cocreate healing. Knowing when to allow Sacred Listening for maximum ease will also be explored in relation to aspects like body language, scent, facial expression, clothing choices, tone of voice, and being still.

On Level Six: *Abundance* (Third Eye Chakra), you start to remember and develop your advanced *sensing* skills to expand your Holistic Healing Business abundance. Once you have more ease communicating who you are as a healer, what you want for your new business, how to direct your HHB actions, and how to connect from your healer's heart, you will need to figure out what to do with all the money, helpful people, and positive experiences you manifest from these alignments! Developing your intuitive capacities on this level will help you shift your growth edge from *struggling* to *sensing* which things to do first, with whom, why, and where. Here you will learn how to graciously harness and harvest as much Universal Assistance as you can aerodynamically carry!

On Level Seven: *Contribution* (Crown Chakra), you explore how creating self-sustaining value through your Holistic Healing Business can ensure its longevity. If you evolve to wanting your HHB to meet and match your Higher Purpose, then this level will guide your Legacy Work, creating holistic full-circle energy to perpetuate a business that benefits many generations beyond you. This level will also help you uncover whether or not your new HHB is in service as a means to another equally awesome end and how to plan for its intentional ending.

After completing this seven level Elevator–Up! process, there are details about how to prepare for an actual launch when that time comes for your HHB. The Business Launch Prep checklist and process may find you ripe for launching your dream business in as little as eight weeks, or you'll just feel a lot clearer about who you are becoming as a healer, what you want from your new business, and exactly when and how you want to get it! You may even find that you have relaxed into just the right amount of allowing versus controlling so that your dream HHB will be mostly "doing" itself while you enjoy "being" the holistic healer you were born to be.

Chapter 4

LEVEL ONE—SECURING CLARITY AND CONFIDENCE TO START YOUR HOLISTIC HEALING BUSINESS

"If you knew who walked beside you at all times on the path that you have chosen, you could never experience fear or doubt again."

– Dr. Wayne Dyer

Much of the success in your HHB journey is about effectively combining things you've already learned and new inspirations that want to express themselves through you to make a greater difference in your world. Let's warm-up your clarity muscles with a twenty-minute exercise developed to help you see how much you already have to "work with" as you are starting your Holistic Healing Business.

Warm-up: Leverage What you Know and Have Right Now

- Begin by setting a timer for ten minutes. Quickly list jobs you've had in the past. Work backwards from any current jobs, as far as you can get in ten minutes. Write down:
  1. Three to five words describing the job
  2. How you were compensated
  3. What service you most enjoyed/best excelled at providing
- Next, with the timer reset for ten more minutes, list the most important thing you learned from each job and, on a scale from one to ten, what your satisfaction level was for each work experience (one being not satisfied, up to ten being very satisfied).
- Finally, review these results daily for this first week to gain clarity about what skills, attitudes, and desires you are bringing to your HHB initiation. Specifically, notice which past work experiences have led you toward or away from an impulse to serve others with your work.

Your Changing Perceptions, Perspectives, and Identity

For years, maybe even decades, you have likely been using other people's rules and measuring sticks to define and validate your professional achievements. One of the greatest pleasures of starting your own Holistic Healing Business is you now have the sacred opportunity to cocreate results that more holistically align with *your* values and vision of success. Now, you get to leverage all your work-related wisdom, lessons, and frustrations to define your authentic value and capacity to meet your client's needs!

One of the first growth edges you are likely to encounter is the fear that you are *definitely* missing something you need *before* you can start your dream HHB. Maybe you think you need to master another modality, acquire the trendiest equipment, or save a certain amount of money for marketing your HHB before it would be wise to launch. Take a few deep breaths and a few minutes to look behind the startup must-haves ricocheting in your mind and note how many of those are based in fear of judgement and/or failure? If you have excelled professionally by meeting expectations defined by others, a lot of your *perceived* self-worth is likely based on following permissions given or withheld by others. Starting your own business creates an opportunity for you to shift the permission energy in your life in a more empowering direction. This can also start to spontaneously heal any chronic blaming habits you may have that will slow down your HHB success. So when you find yourself thinking, "If only they would…" or, "Why do they always…" check in with yourself to see where you are limiting your HHB potential and work freedom by making your empowerment subject to permission from people, places, and forces beyond your control.

Success in your new business will be directly connected to your willingness to continually practice giving *yourself* permission. Thinking and feeling through where you do and don't yet have self-permission in your business can greatly simplify what it means to successfully show up for your clients as you grow. The good news here is that you can learn to *feel* intuitively when you are up against your permission limits. For example, maybe you clench your jaw, hold your breath, or obsess mentally about a pending conversation. The edges of your comfort zones have a purpose that is worth clarifying and exploring so that you can create healthy business boundaries and make conscious, self-loving choices about how you want to grow both your HHB and yourself. As your confidence as a healer grows, self-permission and increased heart-centered connections will naturally unfold. One easy way to start growing your self-permission skills is by practicing *permission to be new* at your business. This includes, but is not limited to, mastering the three humble technologies of:

1. *saying* "I don't know *yet*" (out loud, while smiling)
2. *thinking* "I can do that better next time if I will allow…"
3. *expressing* "I want a better outcome; can we try again?"

When you practice any of these in conversation with your relations, clients, or yourself in the mirror, you are saving precious energy, time, and money, while elevating the emphasis in your HHB efforts from simply making money to also creating *sustainable* value.

Your Evolving Perceptions

Another growth edge awaiting you at your HHB startup will likely be rapid shifts in your perceptions. How you listen, see, feel, and process information and emotions can expand remarkably and rapidly once you start your HHB. Know for sure that your Spirit has been craving this, even if it feels like an ice-cream headache sometimes! Remember the first time you really wanted to have sex and how you felt after the encounter? No matter what happened, your perceptions of yourself sexually became connected to a reality outside of your own head and heart in a very different way than when you were just fantasizing about the sex. Similarly, the energy exchanges involved in starting your own HHB connect you externally in ways that change your understanding of who you are becoming and why you are here.

While starting Inviting Balance in 2000, I had a bit of a "sensory overload" period because everything I now wanted professionally no longer matched the corporate-style life I had successfully created up to that point. On one hand, becoming a professional healer was spiritually liberating and emotionally empowering, and on the other hand, my professional reboot was mentally confusing and physically exhausting. Reflecting on how your sensory and tactile perceptions are shifting is key to developing an understanding of what makes you unique as a being *and* a healer. Tracking these shifts will also greatly enhance and simplify your messaging efforts at Level Five and your abundance expansion work at Level Six. You can journal, video/audio log, or meditate on your evolving sensory experiences to deeply integrate their positive potential on your HHB starting efforts.

After a decade of experimenting with different meditation techniques, I found the Insight Timer app in 2015, and working with it got me over my procrastination speed bump of meditating regularly. Meditating for twenty to thirty minutes a day, five to seven times a week definitely enables me to stay in touch with my evolving perceptions and HHB growth curve.

Lastly, when you think about how specific people, places, and experiences affect your current perceptions of right and wrong or success and failure, do you find yourself focusing mostly on the past, present, or future? Ideally, you will learn to focus on your *current* perceptions, to cocreate the future you've craved for as long as you can remember caring about how you spend your precious professional hours.

Your Expanding Identity

Even if you choose to partner with other healing professionals or movements, you are now shifting into a greater leadership role that gives you a chance to connect more deeply with others through your work experiences. Maybe in the past your work has been just a job and most of your creative and loving energies have flowed through interactions with family, friends, and adventures outside of your work life. As you shift into being a healing space-setter and holder, embracing the potential for experiences of connection, creativity, and service will naturally broaden and likely soften your perspectives in all areas of your life. Your more rigid friends and relations will either adapt and still love you (more), or you will be freed from a whole layer of people who are most likely only interested in using your energy to fulfill their agendas. Try to patiently remember that people generally do what they were taught in relationships, especially comfortable women protecting their status quo. One of the biggest growth lessons I have lived and seen learned by other healers is that your HHB success will be directly proportional to your capacity to not take other people's opinions, intentions, actions, and/or lack of actions personally.

Your Customized Transition Plan

How can you determine the appropriate timeline & energy cost to start your HHB and leave your current work with ease? Just like the wide variety of tempting options available when you pop into your favorite treat shop, there are a multitude of choices for transitioning out of your current work and into the Holistic Healing business of your dreams. How you stick the landing from your exit-leap depends on what your particular life situation requires right now. Most people spend more of their waking hours engaged in work-related activities than any other aspect of their lives, so getting clear about how you want to leave can have a significant *holistic* impact on your HHB starting success and quality of life.

Some common exit choices you may be facing include how to pay your bills until your business is profitable, maintaining your professional reputation, leaving co-workers amicably, wrapping up with work projects, how you will find clients for your new business, and adapting to changes in your daily schedule/structure. Let's dive into these now so you can have a clear plan that addresses your concerns and optimizes your exit *and* transition.

When thinking logically about how to pay your bills while transitioning from your job, common wisdom says to save enough money to cover six to nine months of your fixed living expenses (FLE), plus twelve to eighteen months of your known future business expenses (FBE), plus ten-percent of that sum as a transition emergency fund (TEF)—or (FLE+FBE) x 0.1 = your safe. I have yet to meet anyone who chose to transition exactly this way because saving enough money for a "safe" exit is often an excuse to avoid adding any risk to your career path. Most of the healers I have helped plan through their financial transition usually have more initial success at minimizing financial risk by reorganizing their *spending* habits than their *saving* strategies. Most learn along the way that a lot of their consumption habits were medicating a dissatisfaction with their quality of life that starting their dream HHB helps to rebalance. You can plan for new business expenses in a way that aligns with variables we will quantify in the next two chapters. Most healers I have had the pleasure to cocreate business success with have usually opted for gradual transitions that allow them to maintain some transitional work culture and structure, a part-time income, and potential clients for their emerging HHB.

One client Pam, who thought her employer would be shocked and pissed for leaving her overbooked special events firm, discovered that her boss already guessed she was thinking about leaving. Instead, her boss handed Pam a generous handful of existing clients that she knew loved working with Pam. Her boss did this because she wanted a positive way out of an event planning segment that was now less profitable. While retaining access through a happier Pam to happy clients for more profitable emerging event services she was developing, her boss helped her cocreate a win, win, win. Something to keep in mind here is that job misery rarely exists in a vacuum, and most bosses would secretly rather see their best employees move on if they aren't able to inspire authentic commitment via ongoing growth opportunities for them within their corporation. Many times, I have seen holistic healers sell their

HHB services to their previous employers and several times I have heard about old bosses expressing interest in employment within the new HHB.

Another holistic healer client, Shelly, fantasized about working at her local health food store while she grew her holistic nutrition business. Everyone working there seemed so much more at ease, satisfied and knowledgeable than she despite the fact that she had a Wellness Coaching certification. So, she started working there every other Saturday to see what people were needing and buying. In the first month, she realized that if she let go of her forty-five hour (plus commute time) per week corporate job in town, she would take home more income working twenty-five hours a week at the health food store. Seeing my doubtful eyebrow rise, she excitedly explained that work-related expenses like a "required" separate professional wardrobe, dry cleaning, parking, gas, car wear and tear, tolls, lost family time, commuting, biweekly acrylic nail upkeep, and all the afternoon get-through-it lattes really added up to erode her actual net pay. She also related that those tangible costs ended up being even less important than the priceless work freedom she felt while being more herself at work as a Holistic Healer.

Sometimes you have got to leave your job yesterday. Or maybe your job is changing or ending soon, and you are choosing to make an opportunity out of the timing. Here's a top ten simple, safe, and smart job exit checklist of choices you can use empower your transition with clarity and confidence:

1. Who are the one to three people most effected at work by your leaving in the next two months? What one

thing can you communicate in writing to them within the next two weeks about how you intend to make your exit easier for them? Keep in mind who would make the best reference here, knowing that your coworkers and clients may better speak to your professional attributes than your supervisor.

2. Who can most help you stay connected to the good things you've done and helpful people you've met in your time working there? Be sure to have appropriate and relevant testimonial letters and contact info before you get into the emotional swing of your exit.

3. Who can support you with a loan or investment gift to help cover your financial commitments for a defined business startup period if you have yet to save enough money to leave without financial worry? If you truly must leave now to maintain your integrity without a financial safety net, then you will have the opportunity to learn intuitively that the Universe will provide, and you will adapt, usually in equal measure.

4. What contacts and reSources can you ethically retain from your job that can help you and anyone you are now supporting, financially or otherwise? Experience has shown me that the few competitive or jealous people who begrudge you leaving are insignificant in comparison to the people who will privately and *publicly* respond helpfully to a specific, respectful request to help share info or support your new HHB.

5. What *same* message are you going to say or write, in twenty words or less, about why you are leaving now to

everyone that asks? Can you feel joy in your heart when you say this message in your rear-view mirror before entering the office on the day you intend to give notice?

6. When do you intend to give notice and why then? Can you happily practice said notice with your grandma (or auntie, or elder you respect) and feel like you're telling the truth and being fair?

7. Where are three places you can happily offer your services starting the first of next month? Consider the flexibility and lower overhead of starting out as a mobile service provider if you can safely do so within a distance less than twenty-five miles from home or your current commute, whichever is greater. In most cases, you will need solid internet and phone service to effectively grow your business with ease.

8. How will you uplevel your self-care to align with the challenges of being your own boss and shifting out of your current worktime structure? What do you promise you will do for yourself with your new work freedom? Email or text a list of your top five self-care tips to a bestie or mentor willing to connect with you at least once a week to make sure you are staying well enough to provide quality care to others through your HHB.

9. Why are you *really* still at your job? You don't need to tell anyone else but being honest with yourself will greatly accelerate your easeful and successful exit.

10. How can you let go of any perfectionism tendencies you may be using as a defense strategy that are preventing you from leaving to start your dream HHB? How much

longer are you willing to endure the longing you feel as life is passing you by while you wait for the perfect moment instead of enjoying the relief of just starting from where you are now?

Your Integrous Exit

Being courageous enough to move on from an unsatisfying work life allows your team and company to find someone more inspired to move the company forward with the type of energy you likely had when you started there. The resulting increased alignment with your integrity says more about the importance of your healing services than mere words can express. When you let go and get your HHB started, most of the energy you've had tied up fears and resistance can now be redirected toward gratitude for the honor of serving others in joy from your heart. This uplevel is also a great dose of holistic preventative medicine for living a longer, happier life yourself.

Lastly, because of the personal stress and potential growth that can accompany leaving your job and starting your dream HHB, it is extremely helpful for new HHB business starters to write down the intangible costs and benefits of leaving a regular job *both now and a year out*. Doing this *before* you are in a career transition can give you a written, invaluable detour around self-doubt sink holes and visceral panic plunges. If you are not stopping right now to do this, know that this especially applies to *your* HHB success. This thirty-minute exercise, which clients often discuss over the phone with me, has proven very helpful for the "when to leave" aspect of your exit.

For example, how long will you have access to your current healthcare via your employer? Is there a spousal/domestic partner plan you can better leverage or other free or low-cost government-subsidized health plans you may temporarily qualify for without your current income (www.healthcare.gov/unemployed/coverage/)? How will leaving your job positively or negatively impact your diet, sleep, exercise, and family relationships? If you do this exercise and it is not totally obvious at this time that you, your family, and potential HHB clients have much more to gain by you transitioning as soon as possible, then seriously consider if your HHB is more your Holistic Hobby or your Higher Purpose. Our world is in great need of both Holistic Hobbyists and healers on their mission. Only you know the truth about where your inner compass is pointing you right now. What do you have to lose by getting really clear how you can *best* serve before you start?

If you are committed to drafting or at least outlining a Holistic Healing Business Plan that you will likely use in the first year of your HHB, here is Level One's segment of the work toward accomplishing that by the end of your seven-level process.

Level One Holistic Healing Business Plan Outline Assignment

At Level One, start a document on your device or dedicate a journal to start gathering the pieces you will need to craft your Holistic Healing Business Plan.

This week, note what you know so far about your:

- Main, first focus service of your HHB and its top ten benefits for your ideal client.
- Holistic Healing Business Name—Will people who don't know you easily know what you offer?
- Work Location/s—Consider safety, ADA access, parking, and noise levels during your office hours
- Hours of Operation—When are your ideal clients most available?
- Contact Information—How is your ideal client most easily going to connect and schedule with you? What level of privacy is important for your work-life balance and the safety of you and your relations?

Chapter 5

LEVEL TWO—FOCUSING YOUR DESIRES TO IGNITE YOUR HOLISTIC HEALING BUSINESS

"That which is like; unto itself is drawn"
– **Abraham** through **Ester Hicks**

A s you gain clarity and confidence about how to transition into your dream Holistic Healing Business, you will begin to have more room in your heart and mind to deeply connect with exactly *why* you want to step into a life of holistic service. You may start randomly smiling to yourself or spontaneously making new connections with ideas and feelings you may not have had in a long while, if ever.

As the hope that you have carried with you over the years of finding a better holistic way to be and connect in your world gains intensity, you begin waking in the middle of the night with mysterious, creative whispers. Suddenly, you're talking to yourself in the shower about all kinds of fun and crazy ideas for naming your business and people who will *definitely* help you with your HHB business plan. Fortunately, you are still in the shower, because you've just spontaneously upleveled, and now you and your creative HHB energies have ignited!

Savor and celebrate this ignition, as its embers will linger on in the hearts and spirits of those you elevate with your budding HHB. As the weeks and years pass in your new business development process, you will need to stoke and focus your desires to stay in touch with your deepest creative potential.

Here's a ten- to fifteen-minute warm-up exercise for this second level that you can use whenever you feel numb or scattered in your HHB efforts. I call it The Satisfaction Surrender, and it will elevate your understanding of how knowing what satisfies you can ignite your business creativity and healing results for you and your clients. This focuses your desires by claiming *how much* of *what kind* of successes it would take for you to feel satisfied, and then it helps you surrender to that feeling of satisfaction *now.*

Warm-up: Satisfaction Surrender

- Find a place where you can have privacy with your thoughts and feelings with a journal or phone notes app. Set a timer for five minutes and put across the top of your journal or phone note:

- *I, your favorite name/persona, am deeply satisfied with my HHB startup when*:
  1. List specific outcomes and
  2. Satisfying feelings and
  3. material gains via your HHB efforts
- Keep going until your time sounds…this is where the magic happens!
- Conclude this agreement with your signature and today's date.
- Next, take five to ten minutes to breathe deeply in and out through your mouth while reading aloud to yourself the whole surrender. Make whatever tweaks needed until you feel completely satisfied with the surrender.
- Complete this exercise by closing your eyes and surrendering to the feelings of satisfaction you can *choose* to feel right now until you receive a creative impulse from your subconscious.
- Follow the impulse immediately, even if you just write it down for reflection and action later.

As you lean into this satisfaction surrender exercise with reckless abandon several times over the next week, you will start to see that *focusing* on the emerging emotions and disruptions that you are processing and releasing can create a profound sense of relief and greater space inside you. Track these evolving satisfactions to align with the realest parts of yourself. These are the self-aspects you will want stoked and centered unflinchingly around your *why*, as everything else comes and goes with the negotiations of time.

Over time, these Satisfaction Surrender notes can poignantly highlight where you are prone to abandoning your creativity for comfort. And as you begin to feel safer with the more combustible parts of yourself, you can use this agreement as a Distraction Detox and Anxiety Armor. Whenever you find yourself spinning in confusion or stuck in analysis paralysis, refocusing on your present moment's deepest desires for your HHB will help you realign your efforts with your upleveling integrity as a Holistic Healer. You are essentially teaching your subconscious that it is possible and pleasurable to satisfy your desires, and you can do so for yourself in the privacy of your own power. Knowing from your HHB beginning what it takes to satisfy your HHB aspirations and what that actually feels like *for you* is the secret to keeping your HHB flame alive. We will use these notes later at Level Seven when we delve into your *Sacred Why* and creating sustainable value to ensure your HHB's longevity.

Letting Go of Suffering

As we clear out the fear underbrush and make room for your creative sparks to grow, it's important to *feel* what you will gain by letting go of your current pain and suffering around "work." A few years back, I was working with a man I know affectionately as Pantz-on-Fire Victor. After two months of fantastic but drastic growth, he vanished for over a year. When we reconnected, he calmly related that he had a major shift in his desires for the direction of his life's work as a healer when he realized that he was holding on to the drudgery he experienced running his family's mining business. He thought enduring it made it OK for him to secretly live and love his real purpose as a Healer.

What stories do you have festering deep in your belly about work not being valid and worth compensation unless you are put out of your joy to get it done? So many times, I've heard how a friend's or client's HHB really started to lift off the launch pad when they released the resistance held in their stories about how good work must be hard. The result is a major drain on the exact creative lifeforce you will need to inspire your successful start past the initial euphoria of finding your way out of the corporate cube farm. How willing are you to be a cooperative messenger of healing information and energies? If your currently work in a competitive or combative environment, this vital transition can take time and self-patience. How easy are you willing to let your HHB service work become?

The Extreme Cost of Self-Suppression

Because of the potential negative physical, emotional, mental, and spiritual costs of chronically suppressing desires (*Got Prilosec?*), it is important to develop a few resistance-releasing ninja moves. If you are experiencing numbness in any of these self-aspects, here a few tricks learned from some of my favorite healers and clients over the years. Test out which ones release your particular pressure valves.

1. Rip pages from a phone book while stomping on a hard floor.

2. Practice Kundalini Yoga Breath of Fire for strengthening your nervous system and building stress resistance. Practice for at least a minute every morning.

3. Growl or bark at the tech device or whatever is frustrating you for five to ten seconds.

4. Relax into Hatha Yoga Child's Pose.

5. Have some (safe) hot-mess sex.

6. Inhale Eucalyptus Globulus, neat.

7. Run the dog beside your dirt bike until both of your tongues are slack to one side.

8. Fill your water bottle halfway with ice water and shake it until your arm hurts more than your resistant thought.

9. Exhale a descending whistle and finale with an explosion sound effect that partially escapes your mouth.

10. And my favorite so far…run your tongue as fast as you can along the center seam in the roof of your mouth ten times; then close your eyes and feel the resistance swoosh out the bottom of your feet.

The point here with releasing resistance is that there is no way to get it wrong if you get it done. Your vital creative energy is jammed up behind all that resistance you're holding. Freeing your inner flame from fear and resistance will always help it outshine the darkness of random doubts as you grow your dream HHB.

When I started offering intuitive sessions to some of my regular HHB clients, one of the first downloves that came through was something like, "It's always going to be clearer to first feel your feelings, then intuit your own mind." I always come back to this when I am intuiting which of my client's desires is going to best focus and elevate the issue we have agreed to align around for their session. I also gained the capacity to prime HHB pumps near and far with the A-musing tool. Bringing humor and self-compassion to any unfelt feelings has a muse-attracting magic all its own. Even a smirk or a giggle can gently unseize your creative resistance and keep you moving in the right direction with your HHB desires.

- Simply start by asking yourself what is amusing—or at least interesting—about where you are emotionally in your HHB process right now?
- Did you ever think you would be lucky enough to have a such a quirky issue to resolve?
- What feels ridiculous enough to laugh about in your struggle with this issue?
- Are you taking yourself and your HHB experiments too seriously?

Smile as your Desire Muse shows up and pours a couple shots of *go* juice for you! As you practice using your creative imagination to support your HHB, a more holistic relationship develops between it and your intuitive capacities. We will delve into how imagination and intuition can be two sides of a same coin in Chapter Nine on abundance.

Upleveling Your Point of Attraction

Another reason to stay in touch with your desires is the magnetizing effect aligning with your holistic healing talents can have on all your relationships. Your point of attraction for new clients that best match your service passions is amplified by cultivating clear desires for both yourself and your HHB. Your ideal clients can find you a lot easier if you are consistently affirming this connection and drive to serve them through your *focused* passion and caring. Think about the last time you were inspired by a leader in your everyday life. Was it their offering or charisma you remember being attracted to more? Which of these was more focused and therefore magnetic?

When I connect with a healer that is satisfied and devoted to their offering, I feel more supported in that steadiness and devotion than I do by trending healing modalities. Clear desires uniquely enhance your presence within your client relationships, independent of how you advance or deliver any one particular skill. Spiritual leader Carl W. Buehner captured (and Maya Angelou amplified) this when he said over fifty years ago, "They may forget what you said—but they will never forget how you made them feel."

Learning to Love Your Gaps

Learning to leverage any contrast you feel about where you are now and where you want to go with your HHB is another powerful way to work with your desires. It is a lot easier to fill a gap you are very intimate with than one you try to ignore. The emotional intelligence you can develop from growing through the uncomfortable issues around your new HHB is a valuable skill you can document and model for your clients as you evolve. As you learn how to share holistic problem-solving with your clients, everyone gets a lot more freedom to choose what is right for them in the moment over what they "should" do to play it safe.

A woman named Jenny came to me with intense guilt for spending what she called "family money" on a life-coaching certification program. She said she *should* do something more interesting and helpful with her time as her kids moved away for college. A few weeks into the program, she realized that she just wanted companionship and understanding about grieving her youth and her identity as a mom. She realized that she wouldn't be caught dead hiring a life coach, yet she was now committed financially and contractually to a group of people that seemed really honorable and dedicated to serving as coaches.

As we worked through the contrasts between her desires, guilt, perceived obligations, and repulsions, she was able to see that her shame over needing help was limiting her creative and professional growth. As she worked on the gap between her desires and her pride, she learned firsthand how hard it is for accomplished people to ask for and receive help. This turned out to be her genius in her HHB as a doula for successful couples who get overwhelmed while adopting at-risk infants.

Lastly, staying attuned to you and your client's desires helps you maintain a better balance in your HHB relationships, both inside your sessions and out and about in your community. Knowing what you stand for creates an optimal balance between flexibility and strength with others involved in the success of your HHB.

Now that you have navigated Level Two and started your HHB process around focusing your desires, you can channel some of your creative inspirations and insights into the Level Two segment related HHB business plan assignment. Remember that the authentic passion and enthusiasm you may have overlooked before working this level are exactly the "point of attraction" you may someday harness to fund your HHB above and beyond its starting year.

Level Two Holistic Healing Business Plan Outline Assignment

At Level Two, note or edit what you know so far about your:

- Main, first focus service of your HHB and its top ten benefits for your ideal client
- Holistic Healing Business Name—Will people who don't know you easily know what you offer?
- Work Location/s—Consider safety, ADA access, parking, and noise levels during your office hours.
- Hours of Operation—When are your ideal clients most available?
- Contact Information—How is your ideal client most easily going to connect and schedule with you? What level of privacy is important for your work-life balance and the safety of you and your relations?
- Description of the your HHB (fifty words or less)—What is the main healing service you provide and problem it solves?

- Main goal of your service for self, clients, and other stake holders—What's your HHB *why*?

Chapter 6

LEVEL THREE—CREATING CLEAR INTENTIONS TO POWER YOUR HOLISTIC HEALING BUSINESS

"It takes at least five years of rigorous training to be spontaneous."

– **Martha Graham**, Modern Dance Founder

As we begin sorting out all the business building intentions and resulting actions that will most powerfully fuel your HHB start-up efforts, it is good to get grounded around what your ego is up to in the process to keep it (you) aligned with your HHB. This exercise is designed to help you identify any chronic judgements, ignorance, and arrogance that may be handicapping your ability to sustain your best holistic healer's mindset.

51

Warm-up: Collaborate with your Ego for Clarity

- Start by picking a day this week to have some fun observing yourself.

- The night before, take five to ten sticky notes and draw an up arrow on each that reminds you of an elevator up button. Next, stick them in your high traffic places like your bathroom mirror, wallet, fridge door, car rearview mirror, desk, computer, cellphone case, etc.

- As you move through your day, use the sticky notes to notice what you are thinking about when you see them. When you find yourself thinking an arrogant thought or bickering with your ego, reach out and press the up symbol you drew, close your eyes (egoballs), and imagine getting on an elevator with your ego. Ask your ego to take that thought up to the next level and show you its purpose in the present moment.

- As you see the elevator doors open in your mind's eye, enjoy how clever and helpful your ego can be when it's invited to collaborate for your greater clarity.

Uplevel Your Healing Gifts with Clear Intention Setting

Clarity can be elusive and fickle if you're making business decisions without first setting clear intentions. If you are drawn to holistic healing because of a life-changing experience you cocreated with a healer that helped you, those experiences can create context around your services that your clients can relate to authentically, so don't be afraid to let your own experiences shape your HHB intentions. Knowing what decisions to make and actions to do first is also simplified by prioritizing your intentions after you set them.

Let's start by creating a list of some of the physical outcomes you intend to help your clients obtain as they receive healing through you. You may already know clearly that you are drawn to one or a few body systems more than others. The eleven systems of the body are the integumentary, muscular, skeletal, nervous, circulatory, lymphatic, respiratory, endocrine, urinary/excretory, reproductive, and digestive. Notice as you are making this list which systems seem weaker or stronger in your own body temple. When I was in my final clinics for Massage Therapy school in 2001, one of my mentors pointed out that it's natural to give the massage that your body is craving. You will discover how your own body, subconscious, and Source will speak to you when you consciously set holistic healing body-function-centered intentions that reflect your own healing needs, learning, and goals. Consider that the clearer and more cared for you are as a conduit of healing from Source, the better your HHB beginning and client satisfaction will be.

The first and sometimes only question I ask a client at the beginning of our sessions is "How do you want to feel when we are done with our session today?" This very practical, grounding, open-ended question empowers them to show and tell me how to set crystal clear intentions *with them* around phenomena that are often unseen and unclear to them before this inquiry. As the holistic service provider, how do you want to feel while you are working with your clients and when the session is complete? This will also inform and uplevel how you set effective *emotional* intentions for your dream HHB. As human beings, we have all felt a wide range of emotions. They are a very powerful shared information system between you and your client that can greatly enhance what you both get out of your time together. I know a Reiki Master named Kim who says that because she always asks her clients if and *where* they feel any emotions as she is working, her many repeat clients know what to expect emotionally in their sessions. They also have permission to communicate freely about the emotional information as it arises.

One way to quantify your *intellectual* intentions for your HHB in general and your client experiences specifically, is to get clear about what you want to learn and teach while upleveling your Healing Gifts. When you stay open to teaching others about the healing you have had the privilege of 'downloving' through your HHB, you may notice a substantial increase in cooperation and compliance from your clientele. Most people who strive to understand and apply the Law of Attraction (www.abraham-hicks.com) will be supportive of your mental intention to uplevel your Healing Gifts to secure a more holistic life and the means to earn a living through sharing them.

As your listening and intuitive empathic skills develop through your holistic work, you will be more able to naturally discern and reflect back to your clients what you think they are wanting to learn and heal in your work together. Taking the time to intentionally glean this will also give you information necessary for practicing your pattern recognition skills. For example, after several years of giving regular Q&A Intuitive Sessions, I started to notice certain behavioral and phenomena patterns around the clients who were accessing their intuition directly in our sessions versus those who were passively asking questions and listening to responses. When I ask them if they want to know how I sense them doing this, they almost always say, "Absolutely!" It is usually tremendously validating for them to have their patterns and unconscious connecting witnessed and detailed. Because I set the clear intellectual intention to recognize these patterns in my HHB, I was able to develop a more holistic intuitive style and a whole new intuitive training program for guiding people to remember and develop their own intuitive gifts.

Experience and Emanate the *In All Ways* Consciousness

My favorite HHB intentions to set are ones related to the *spiritual* aspect of holistic healing. This stratum of intentions is where I tend to help healers find their 'power tool' intentions as we enlist and align with the Unseen. This is where I see clients and healers truly being met where they are. Ancestors, Angel guides, Jesus, Buddha, Krishna, Allah, Nanak, Source Energies, oracle cards, 'aumakua, plant devas, etc. don't seem to care so much about the *how* of healing as other more tangible messengers and modalities that can be bound by the mental limitations, egos, fears, and common beliefs about the nature of our shared physical realms.

When your spiritual intentions are clear and yield the appropriate permissions, miracles become a natural, safe, and upleveling aspect of your HHB. Make a Sacred Space to know where you stand with the spiritual intentions underpinning you HHB, and you will gift everyone you encounter with the inspiration to do the same. Discuss with a wide variety of positive people what, if any, distinctions you make between spirituality and religion in your work. That way, when your clients inevitably ask, you will be calm, clear, and respectful in relating around this often-divisive topic. This will also help you joyfully and confidently set your HHB spiritual intentions.

One of my most profound and treasured HHB uplevels occurred while I was 'downloving' the Intuitive Expansion Training series in 2010. As I set the spiritual intention to cocreate a system to help people remember and develop their inherent intuitive Gifts, I experienced a long, peaceful silence akin to being under still water. Then I discerned the message, 'This offering, per their requests, is brought with and through the *In All Ways* Consciousness.'... All righty then! I have come to recognize the frequency of this message every time I hear the sentiment 'with Love, all things are possible.' As you set your HHB spiritual intentions, you can experiment with the In All Ways Consciousness by asking yourself what are all the ways clients can receive healing through your HHB.

Document Intentions to Up-level Your Decision-Making and Sustaining Powers

Your sacred clients are worth every notation, and the materialization of your dream HHB depends on your increasing capacity to commit to and refine clear intentions. Here's an intention setting exercise you can work with throughout Level Three to help capture and commit to your physical, emotional, mental, and spiritual intentions for HHB. Note—it is really powerful to gain awareness of any conflicts between various intentions. It may simply mean that you have different intentions in different situations. This is a lot easier to see when you document them:

- What are the three most important holistic *emotional* outcomes for your HHB (and therefore clients), and in what order can you see yourself achieving them?
- What are the three most tangible holistic *physical* outcomes for your dream HHB in the first year, and which one is the most inspiring for you right now?
- What are three *mindsets* you see challenging people you care about, and how does your awareness of these mindsets benefit those receiving your holistic services?
- What are the three most important holistic *spiritual* outcomes you would like to be a part of elevating humanity with as you look back at the end of your life?

Once you have clear answers to these questions and any others that come up while you are exploring, you can more clearly set empowering intentions that give your holistic services context and your clients more value for the trust, time, and money they are investing in your collaboration.

- Look back over your answers and highlight or underline words that generate action. For example, "I intend to *journal for at least 30 minutes a week* on what my clients are teaching me through our cocreative healing experiences."
- Lastly, draft a list of your top five to ten most inspiring intentions that you can polish and uplevel your Healing

Gifts through as you watch your unique HHB services and processes develop.

Once you have your delectable list of top five to ten intentions for your HHB, I highly recommend prioritizing them in a way that feels like you are inviting balance between your mind, body, and spirit. So, make a point to read your intentions at least once daily, and notice if you are tending to all parts of yourself in a reasonably balanced way. If you really want to lean into some bombastic magic with HHB intention setting, record yourself passionately speaking your prioritized intentions, then listen to yourself any time you think you are stuck or confused with your HHB decisions. Any resistance you feel about intention setting may just be normal resistance to change. You can revisit the resistance releasing techniques in the previous chapter to gain some freedom from your fears/ resistance.

True Balance Requires More Flexibility Than Strength

Inviting balance between your body, feelings, thoughts, intentions, and Source generates a very powerful point of attraction for your HHB clients. A quick story about balance: when I arrived at the University of Maryland in 1992, I secretly decided that, alongside my primary degree, I would also get a degree in Modern Dance. I thought this would keep me in shape and away from the various collegiate bong options, all while not rocking the boat with my family's expectations about getting a 'real degree.'

All my life, my deepest yearning was to be a dancer, but I believed that I was too late to catch up with all the others who spent their childhood in tights, fretting over two extra pounds. I ran myself ragged by my sophomore year, and I asked a trusted teacher how I could possibly balance all this while maintaining my health and grades. He smiled knowingly and pointed with his chin toward another dancer warming up on stage, her body uplit in neon blue. He asked me what I thought of her ability to balance the strenuous posture she was practicing.

He then pointed out that if I look closer, I could see that the balance she was maintaining was managed by countless, minute adjustments she was able to make because of how many times she had navigated that very specific alignment. Intentions can be very much the same. When you trod the path of them regularly, making subtle but crucial adjustments in alignment with your inner compass, balance becomes increasingly spontaneous and organic—but never stagnant or still. What I encourage healing arts practitioners to remember about balance when they are initiating holistic adventures is to keep in mind that staying in a *sustainable* balance is much more attainable with *flexibility* than *rigidity*.

Sometimes when I guide an intention-setting process with someone, we need it to be a little bit simpler and a lot more fun, so l suggest the "Inner Staff Meeting" game to understand the intentions of their current HHB inner-staff. The goal here is to discover what you are aligned and misaligned about *internally* so that you can tamp down a lot of the mental spinning that can come up, especially when committing to intentions seems challenging.

Here's how to play. With your eyes closed and a phone voice recorder app live on your phone, call an impromptu Inner Staff Meeting of all the different characters that tend to talk in your head when you focus on your HHB. In ten minutes, quickly detail for the recording the size of the room, shape of the table, who is there, and what's the main concern or intention they are each repeating. It is mind blowing how many different opinions you can be spending your intention-setting energy on before you even talk to anyone outside of your own head.

Typically, with this clarity game, there is a boss that's running the meeting, someone texting under the table, one or more bored notetakers, a toddler or young child complaining, and lots of cross talking. Having a recording of this and listening to it daily at this level while you are developing your intention setting can be both entertaining and healing. Worth their weight in gold for your HHB bottom line, clear intention setting skills are going to inform and fuel your best business decisions and actions. At a minimum, it becomes a lot clearer by what repetitive messages are coming from which characters, where you are setting your HHB intentions from "should's" and past fears. Priceless.

Another benefit of setting and frequently visiting clear intentions at your HHB beginning is that you gain awareness of how your daily business efforts are either expending or expanding your energy, also known as HHB fuel. When you keep an eye on your intentions fuel gauge, it is much easier to see how you're expending this energy than when you are running on or close to empty energetically.

Also, have you thought though how you are going to navigate *doing* your business while *being* present in satisfying ways with your clients? Check your drafted intentions to see if they reflect an effort on your part to balance being and doing. After wading through this intention setting process repeatedly with both friends and clients, I have learned that people who prioritize, or at least acknowledge, the importance of this balance seem to develop a greater capacity for listening and empathy. They prove better at letting the work get mostly done *through* them *by* their clients instead of *for* their clients *by* them. This is akin to teaching someone how to understand their own inner compass versus telling them where to go based on your understanding of their map.

Let's wrap up your Level 3 uplevel by briefly drafting your HHB *Launch Manifesto* about how you want to feel when you have launched your Holistic Healing Business. Take ten to fifteen minutes right now to quickly write down your ideal feelings, thoughts, and sensing states at the moment you decide your HHB is successfully launched. Write it in first person, present tense, and include at least one element that represents your emotional, physical, mental, and spiritual self-aspects each. Now that you have all this mojo and meaning written down, it's time to pause and celebrate the sheer willpower and holistic caring you have exercised by actually showing up for your HHB intention setting. Across all walks of life, it is a known phenomenon that written intent is ninety five percent more likely to yield desired results than just hanging out with great but unwritten ones in your head. Below is the Level Three HHB Business Plan assignment for you to practice intention-based decision making with this week. Next week, we will be feeling into your ideal balance between heart and will with your dream-coming-true Holistic Healing Business.

Level Three Holistic Healing Business Plan Outline Assignment

At Level Three, note or edit what you know so far about your:

- Main, first focus service of your HHB and its top ten benefits for your ideal client
- Holistic Healing Business Name—Will people who don't know you easily know what you offer?
- Work Location/s—Consider safety, ADA access, parking, and noise levels during your office hours.
- Hours of Operation—When are your ideal clients most available?
- Contact Information—How is your ideal client most easily going to connect and schedule with you? What level of privacy is important for your work-life balance and the safety of you and your relations?
- Description of the your HHB (fifty words or less)— What is the main healing service you provide and problem it solves?
- Main goal of your service for self, clients, and other stake holders—What's your HHB *why*?

- Description of your three closest perceived competitors. Focus on defining just the facts related to their who, what, when, where, why, and how. Researching this info will be critical to your capacity to harmonize, cooperate, and collaborate professionally in your chosen arena.

Chapter 7

LEVEL FOUR—ENCOURAGING CONNECTION TO SUSTAIN YOUR HOLISTIC HEALING BUSINESS

"In every community, there is work to be done. In every nation, there are wounds to heal. In every heart, there is the power to do it."

– Marianne Williamson

In our first level, we explored together how your feelings and thoughts provide invaluable information that helps you gain clarity and confidence in yourself and your HHB startup process. Next, we focused your desires for your business to help ground your inspiration and internal commitment. With this foundation of clarity, confidence, and inspiration, we then began to set intentions and unfold decisions, actions, and directions that align with the upleveling holistic healer you are remembering yourself to be.

On this fourth level, we are enjoying some early fruits of the personal work you have moved through as we start to consider how you want to handle a very profound crossroads in your HHB development process.

Warm-up: Where do you feel gratitude?

- Set aside ten minutes, put your phone in airplane mode, and get comfortably seated with your eyes closed and hands relaxed.

- Breathe deeply and feel your chest expand and naturally rebound.

- Recall one person, one place, and one thing you are grateful for from this past week.

- Cycle gently between the three images of the chosen person, place, and thing until you can locate where in your physical body you tangibly feel your gratitude for them.

- As you cycle through these three images, notice if your physical experience of gratitude remains consistent or shifts around in your body.

- Now choose the image that gives you the strongest felt sense of gratitude and focus on its body location for three relaxing breaths. Give this gratitude space within you a sacred name like "Heart Center" or "Love Lounge."

- Next, feel the words "Thank You" in that space and let it go with a deep breath in through your nose and out your mouth.
- Complete by rolling your shoulders with your breath three or four times before opening your eyes and returning to the flow of your day.

If you feel disconnected, lonely, or unsupported as you are working through your HHB efforts, repeat the name of your gratitude space until you can reconnect with and physically feel gratitude there again.

How Much Heart Connection Will You Bring?

Ultimately, your business successes will rely heavily on how much heart you are willing to bring to your everyday connections with the people, places, and experiences your HHB will naturally intersect you with. No matter how much you enjoy solitude or prefer to develop most of your offering alone, your value and meaning is amplified by how open-heartedly you can embrace your appropriate and authentic connections to the healing community around you and your emerging HHB. Beyond wanting to be a good global citizen or provide the right service to your ideal clients, there is a very special commUnity support and connection that generating an HHB can bring to your life journey.

While your HHB Higher Purpose and your Higher Purpose as a healer are clearly connected and ideally harmonious, your HHB now has the potential to self-perpetuate through your clients and the potential community around your Healing Gifts. Practically speaking, learning how to contribute to your larger community yields many tangible and intangible benefits. Some healers discover powerful patterns in the healing work they do in groups versus amongst those they have guided individually. Your clients may be naturally attracted to work cooperatively as they discover and uplevel their Gifts. You may see this model trending in your area, such as when a popular yoga teacher steps up to offer yoga teacher trainings or when an art therapist hosts a weekly podcast with guest speakers on your local community station. They are remembering people of like-mindedness and heart to elevate their client connections *while* marketing their services.

When many people are focusing their energy together to live their common values, aligning with your Higher Purpose can become more inspired and achievable. Even if you prefer to keep your healing service "small batch" or "local brew," creating the opportunity for select clients to become members of a healing community or movement you facilitate and lead is a great contribution you have the privilege to consider at this level. Keep in mind that there are many progressive holistic healing movements that you can simply refer your clients to when they ask, and they will ask!

In 2007, Clarion Sphere Intuitive Gatherings were re-membered in my HHB evolution when a small handful of my clients asked me to do group intuitive gatherings that rotated between their venues and homes. These gatherings continue to this day and focus on a healing topic that directs and harmonizes all the energies. To create these dynamic spheres of healing group energy, sacred space is set and then info on a preselected topic is downloved for fifteen to twenty minutes. Then questions are asked of the Source energies present so that empowering answers and healing energies can be transmitted. Afterward, members of these intuitive gatherings have the added benefit of interacting around their experiences, which creates community for them.

It is one of my proudest healer contributions that many Sphere Builders have gone on to work together on various holistic endeavors for the Highest Good of All. A few of them have also become trusted personal friends over the last five to ten years. The key word here is *few*. Initially, my personal friend/client boundaries were much more porous, and I felt like an intuitive vending machine most of the time. When I began to understand codependency (https://melodybeattie.com/books/) and what I was getting out of it, I made the heart-centered choice to share friend time only with positive people who were committed to developing their own inner compasses and that lean toward light-hearted and positive ways of being.

How to Build Your Holistic Healing Business on *Love* versus *Fear*

You may feel surprised or overwhelmed by the ever-expanding number and variety of decisions you have made in just the first four levels of your Elevator-Up! journey. Hopefully, you are already able to track how looking at your fears, desires, and intentions for your HHB has you falling more in love with your new work freedoms with every decision you navigate. It's helpful at this point to go deeper in your awareness of where you tend to hang out on the emotional spectrum between Love and Fear.

You likely already know that your primitive brain is hard wired to avoid change. So, even if you have the clearest path forward in your mind, stay aware of how the basic fear of change can find you occasionally stuck in thinking or acting from fear. Let's connect with some ways you can keep upleveling by leaning into the direction of love as you work though the multiple growth edges and changes inherent to sustaining your new HHB. In contrast, when you are having a joyful time making decisions and cocreating healing experiences with your clients, you have the opportunity to put some of those good healing memories someplace special for the times when you may feel less connected and supported in your efforts. Give your creative inner child a little space at this level to craft a healing memories scrap book, blog, treasure box, or jingle. The more senses you involve, the more opportunities you will have to reconnect with your best HHB successes whenever you want or need to.

Also, keeping your HHB potential client pipeline full enough so that you don't notice when people opt-out is a powerful gift to yourself and the clients that opt-in. When you are shifting your energy around your work life from meeting productivity goals set mostly by others to self-directing your daily activities, it is important to be connecting with positive people and activities in your community. Keeping your positive activity pipeline full helps you focus on all the new things you are brave enough to be trying. When you consistently plant enough seeds in your garden, you have lots of beautiful growth to focus on instead of what's eating your tomatoes. For ideas on how to keep your HHB positive pipeline full of meaningful, business building actions, visit www.invitingbalance.com/reSources.

Developing Heart-Centered Outreach and Healing Community to Support Your HHB

One powerfully loving way to create a community around your HHB is to consciously create an energy of *pull* vs *push* in your outreach/marketing efforts. If you have ever been involved in standard marketing efforts with mainstream businesses before, you are likely used to the model of telling your clients what they need and shouting over all the options to aggressively "grab their eyeballs." You now have the chance with your own HHB to emanate your message about your services in a way that creates a loving invitation instead of a fear/scarcity-based call to action. You can start the shift from push to pull in your new HHB client outreach by taking the benefits you've listed for your main service and turning them into the questions your ideal client is looking for the answers to. For example, your social media posts and website blogs might emphasize the question, "Are you tired of feeling tired? versus highlighting that the main benefit of your lead service is "increased energy." The most important pull you can create for aligning with your ideal clients is emanating the belief that there are plenty of clients to go around and that you are inviting quality service relationships over quantity.

Growing More Courage for Your HHB

On my thirtieth birthday, my mom gave me a really important gift. We were on the phone and I was fretting about how frustrated I felt at nine months in to starting my HHB that no one in my current social or work circles seemed to really get why I was risking so much professionally to create my own HHB. I wanted them to see how important the work I was doing was for the greater good and give me respect and encouragement. She gruffly huffed back at me, "Why do you care what they think? You should know by now that people can't even see what you're up to because they are too busy focusing on themselves. You might as well just do whatever you want."

While this was not exactly the loving, maternal feedback I was prodding for, it did stop my complaining long enough for me to realize that my fear of what my friends and clients thought of me was limiting my business bravery and growth, as well as stifling my love affair with my new HHB. The word "courage" translates roughly as 'time for heart.' When helping healers transcend their early HHB growth edges, I see massive improvements in their courage by coaching them through what they feel in their heart they *can* do right now, instead of what they are afraid of trying. Like any other skill, practice makes progress *and* helps with anxiety relief, self-confidence, and increased capacity to be vulnerable.

Another very special and courageous role that healers grow into as they start to see just how much healing can happen in the safe space of a community of like hearts and minds is creating sanctuary. Discerning whether a client needs *immediate,* appropriate sanctuary and connection or gradual relationship development, can help you avoid getting into codependent dynamics with clients in acute crisis. By participating in a network of support providers in your chosen community, you have a lot more options when someone comes to you in great suffering. Many healers fall into the trap that they should know how to take care of every pain and challenge that a client presents. I've seen a lot of spiritual egotism emerge when competitive healers try to work without a network of trusted peers and mentors. Someday, you will be likely a mentor to other newer healers, but in your HHB beginnings, you have the great opportunity to experience a wide variety of healing approaches and results through *aligned referring*. It is a unique and priceless opportunity to witness the cooperative magic of what moves through holistic healing approaches that prioritize client needs.

Also, when your clients see you are connected to and have a working knowledge of other valuable holistic healing reSources they might need, you have a much greater chance of creating a long-term empowered relationship with them. People love having lots of choices almost as much as the *really* love having someone they trust to help them make their best choice with them. Another benefit of authentically participating in a healing services network is that it rapidly accelerates the percentage of your business that comes to you via qualified referral. Think about the times you have been vulnerable enough to try a new healing service. Did you randomly select a provider, or did you seek a referral from someone you trust and respect?

Building Community Connections with Events

Consider attending and serving at other people's events and retreats before offering your own. Events can be and feel radically different on the ground than they do on their promotional websites or in social media posts. By helping out at a wide variety of healing events, you may get your own needs for connection and validation met while you figure out what the community around your HHB needs from a potential event you will host. It is important to let the event host know that your intention for helping is to understand how to best host your own events eventually. You may be amazed at how someone who has dealt with time-sensitive event logistics is willing to share helpful info that can make your event really effective for your community of like-minds.

When I decided to travel the US west in an RV to find out what kinds of potential events matched my ideal client's needs, I learned the difference between having a lovely yoga wardrobe and helping groups of thirty to one-hundred strangers safely access their inner strength with yoga and intuitive skills training. Come to find out, my capacity to be and stay present in a ninety-minute class or workshop was way more important in their hearts than how well I technically demonstrated the postures and techniques.

Two and a half years later, when I finally came off the road and settled in Hawai'i, I had gained more understanding of how to best *serve* by *serving* at a wide variety of events and roles while on the road. I learned what people most wanted was to feel unity with others at the events. They were not so much paying for the vegan food we served or the green venue amenities. They most valued the connections and transcendent interpersonal experiences they believed were most accessible to them at these festivals and holistic events. As I plan events now, these priceless experiences help me create value that is connection-based, so that the event always has enough meat on its bones to keep people satisfied in their *choice* to engage in the community around my HHB.

When you encourage and allow your HHB to grow within a community of other service-oriented providers, you get to enjoy being infused regularly with the *in all ways* consciousness. This means that when someone comes to you in trust for healing support, your baseline perspective is "let's figure out together a few choices for your healing, and then I can support you in making your best choice right now." When you only fly solo in your HHB services, there is a tremendous temptation to impose your most comfortable or preferred healing methods to every client problem. If you can keep an open mind to networking, you will likely offer clients much more by staying active in a community of wellness reSources that you and your clients may not have even known exists.

Another option you can explore if you are curious about other healing service providers outside your immediate community is to create your business network in a different community than the one you live in. Distance has its own set of challenges, but some of my clients starting HHBs who met resistance in their hometown thrived by finding and supporting their tribe outside of the zone where their children attended school, spouses worked, and pastors preached. The idea here is that if you find yourself in a community that needs more time to understand who you are and how you are a force for The Highest Good of All (HGA), then don't force it. Stay open to getting your community connection needs met where people are actively seeking your particular healing genius. No matter what you heart prefers as you uplevel your HHB connections, if you focus this week on how you want to feel in your HHB relationships, you will start to spontaneously and gently align the right people, places, and experiences. Then, you can choose what's right for your heart and the heart of your potential HHB community.

For this week's additions to your HHB business plan, you will be focusing on what other holistic connections would be uplifting *for your ideal clients*. As you practice opening your heart and mind to cocreating a cooperative care model through your HHB, take courage in knowing that you will be freeing your clients from needless suffering, confusion, wasted time, energy, and costs creating some sustainable healing connections on everyone's behalf!

Level Four Holistic Healing Business Plan Outline Assignment

At Level Four, note or edit what you know so far about your:

- Main, first focus service of your HHB and its top ten benefits for your ideal client.
- Holistic Healing Business Name—will people who don't know you easily know what you offer?

- Work Location/s—consider safety, ADA access, parking, and noise levels during your office hours.

- Hours of Operation—when are your ideal clients most available?

- Contact Information—How is your ideal client most easily going to connect and schedule with you? What level of privacy is important for your work-life balance and the safety of you and your relations?

- Description of the your HHB (fifty words or less)— What is the main healing service you provide and problem it solves?

- Main goal of your service for self, clients, and other stake holders—What's your HHB *why*?

- Description of your three closest competitors: focusing on their who, what, when, where, why and how.

- Describe members of your current or future dream team for your HHB. Try imagining a group of two to ten healers that have more complimentary than perceived competitive services. What circle of providers would your ideal client most benefit from having aligned on one support team? For example, in 2000 I was an Office Manager at Crossings Center for the Healing Traditions (http://crossingshealing.com) while I was in Massage Therapy school nearby. Their approach, which is still thriving twenty years later, is to offer each client a *care team* and healing options versus just acupuncture or holistic nutrition.

Chapter 8

LEVEL FIVE—COMMUNICATING AUTHENTICALLY TO STRENGTHEN YOUR HOLISTIC HEALING BUSINESS

"When the trust account is high, communication is easy, instant, and effective."
– Stephen R. Covey

As you uplevel your self-awareness and start practicing conscious communication skills that reflect your authentic style as a Holistic Healer, your outreach will gain momentum as you are able to communicate with more ease and consistency about your HHB.

Warm-up

Complete this simple, but intensely healing communication exercise three to five times by yourself until you intuitively remember who you want to try doing it with.

- Begin by finding a naturally or softly lit mirror where you can see yourself from at least the waist up
- With a timer set for one minute, meet your own gaze, smile, and put your fingertips on the mirror's surface.
- Breath more deeply than normal, in and out through your mouth, and simply focus on your breath while you gently smile at your own reflection.
- At the end of a minute, gently close your eyes, breathe as deeply as possible in through your nose and let whatever sound is there waiting there ride your exhale through your mouth.
- Next, open your eyes and see what is clearer to you now; speak that truth to yourself quietly and keep your fingertips connected with your reflection's fingertips.
- Once you are able to do this for a minute, consider allowing a trusted partner to be your mirror. With eyes connected and fingertips touching, breath and smile together. Decide before you start who will share first, while the other remains silent and open.

Building up the amount of time you can simply watch yourself or another breathe without losing authentic connection helps you develop your capacity to harness the healing power of being present in the moment.

Sacred Listening and Empathetic Relating

Cultivating your ability to be quietly present speaks a thousand words to your HHB clients about your capacity to respect the natural rhythms of their healing processes. Two empowering skills that can save you countless hours of misaligned effort, while rapidly improving your service skills and the joy factor of delivering them, are *Sacred Listening* and *Empathetic Relating*. You know the relief you experience when someone can hear you, without interrupting or reacting? Marry that with a cold drink of cucumber mint water on a hot desert day, and you are close to the feeling the benefit Sacred Listening can provide both you and your client. Most people are conditioned to listen for cues that help them formulate a response that will get them closer to *their* desired outcome, which is not only energetically limiting, but it doesn't usually work without a lot of confusing mental gymnastics. There is a competitive nature to most pedestrian listening that can be very jarring when your client has an expectation that you will hear them fully as a unique being before attempting to apply any predetermined healing modality. Modalities can be awesome communication containers and energy elevators when in a healer's hands and heart that is treating all client communication elements as Sacred.

When I asked a bodyworker named Emmy why she wasn't taking any new clients last year, she told me that she got much better at listening to what people *weren't* saying and what they were doing with their body language. Because of this, she started working more deeply with a small number of existing clients, guiding them through other areas than they initially came to her for.

The good and challenging news of Sacred Listening is that each interaction requests a slightly different combination of listening variables. What I know so far is that if you practice noticing your client's breathing over time, the set of their shoulders, their level of eye tension, their hand and foot gestures, and where they put the pauses in their stream of words, you have an extraordinary chance of catching a Sacred Listening wave with them.

Empathetic Relating is the exhalation to Sacred Listening's inhalation. Once you have fully received what the being in front of you is sharing with their words, intonation, and body language, you have an equal opportunity for mirroring. You can reflect information and emotion back to them in a way that they can't see when it's in their emotional and spiritual blind spots. It's like when someone is really into getting an itch on their back scratched that they can't quite reach. Normal listening is like telling them to rub there back against the corner of the bookcase and Empathetic Relating is immediately reaching into those blind spots, holding *their* backscratcher near their hand and asking with your eyes, "Is this what you're looking for right now'?

In 2014, I accepted an incredible opportunity to work at a Permaculture Conscious Community on the Big Island of Hawai'i. I was there to prepare meals from the food we grew and teach yoga for twenty two people attending a sustainable agricultural workshop. Immediately, I noticed that most of them were amplifying their healing service messaging and connections with all sorts of variations of Marshall Rosenberg's Non-Violent Communication (NVC) technique. Also known as Compassionate Communication (CC), this technique works with lists of needs/feelings to cultivate safe communication that is inherently effective at the spiritual level for all who are willing to connect through it.

Because healers tend to be communication enthusiasts, I find these two lists really helpful when beginning an HHB and integrating a lot of new client relationships. Staying grounded in common needs and feelings is what I think Rosenburg was getting at with this highly organized and empathetic communication option. When you are willing to look for the needs connected to the feelings you and your new clients are navigating, you have a greater common ground for seeing what's at the heart of the desire for healing. A woman named Sarah in this community also taught me that if you practice NVC/CC with roughly the same group of people over time, you'll be able to see basic communication patterns of feelings and their related needs across all people. I wonder what a field study of that might yield for dissolving barriers between groups of people that think their feelings and needs are too different for common understanding to be possible?

Here are the Compassionate Communication Feelings and Needs (NVC/CC) lists that can help you communicate your HHB message more authentically and consistently. As you elevate your ability to stay more present with conscious communication techniques, you strengthen the messages that you use to connect with your HHB clients, partners and communities. Maintaining consistent messages about your

Healing Gifts builds client and community trust you can grow your unique HHB brand through.

NVC/CC Feelings List

These words can be used when we want to express a combination of emotional states and physical sensations. This list is neither exhaustive nor definitive. It is meant as a starting place to support anyone who wishes to engage in a process of deepening self-discovery and to facilitate greater understanding and connection between people.

There are two parts to this list: feelings we may have when our needs are *being met* and feelings we may have when our needs are *not being met*.

Feelings when your needs *are satisfied* sorted into general categories:

Affectionate

- Compassionate
- Friendly
- Loving
- Openhearted
- Sympathetic
- Tender
- Warm

Confident

- Empowered
- Open
- Proud
- Safe
- Secure

Engaged

- Absorbed
- Alert
- Curious
- Enchanted
- Engrossed
- Entranced
- Fascinated
- Interested
- Intrigued

- Involved
- Spellbound
- Stimulated

Excited

- Amazed
- Animated
- Ardent
- Aroused
- Astonished
- Dazzled
- Eager
- Energetic
- Enthusiastic
- Giddy
- Invigorated
- Lively
- Passionate
- Surprised
- Vibrant

Exhilarated

- Blissful
- Ecstatic
- Elated
- Enthralled
- Exuberant
- Radiant
- Rapturous
- Thrilled

Grateful

- Appreciative
- Moved
- Thankful
- Touched

Hopeful

- Expectant
- Encouraged
- Optimistic

Inspired

- Amazed
- Awed
- Wonder

Joyful

- Amused
- Delighted
- Glad
- Happy
- Jubilant
- Pleased
- Tickled

Peaceful

- Calm
- Clear headed
- Centered
- Comfortable
- Content
- Equanimous

- Fulfilled
- Mellow
- Quiet
- Relaxed
- Relieved
- Satisfied
- Serene
- Still
- Tranquil
- Trusting

Refreshed
- Enlivened
- Rejuvenated
- Renewed
- Rested
- Restored
- Revived

Feelings when your needs are *not satisfied*, sorted into general categories:

Afraid
- Apprehensive
- Dread
- Foreboding
- Frightened
- Mistrustful
- Panicked
- Petrified
- Scared
- Suspicious
- Terrified
- Wary
- Worried

Annoyed
- Aggravated
- Disgruntled
- Dismayed
- Displeased
- Exasperated
- Frustrated
- Impatient
- Irritated
- Irked

Angry
- Enraged
- Furious
- Incensed
- Indignant
- Irate
- Livid
- Outraged
- Resentful

Aversion

- Animosity
- Appalled
- Contempt
- Disgusted
- Dislike
- Hate
- Horrified
- Hostile
- Repulsed

Confused

- Ambivalent
- Baffled
- Bewildered
- Dazed
- Hesitant
- Lost
- Mystified
- Perplexed
- Puzzled
- Torn

Disconnected

- Alienated
- Aloof
- Apathetic
- Bored
- Cold
- Detached
- Distant
- Distracted
- Indifferent
- Numb
- Removed
- Uninterested
- Withdrawn

Disquiet

- Agitated
- Alarmed
- Discombobulated
- Disconcerted
- Disturbed
- Perturbed
- Rattled
- Restless
- Shocked
- Startled
- Surprised
- Troubled
- Turbulent
- Turmoil
- Uncomfortable
- Uneasy
- Unnerved
- Unsettled
- Upset

Embarrassed

- Ashamed
- Chagrined

- Flustered
- Guilty
- Mortified
- Self-conscious

Fatigue

- Beat
- Burnt out
- Depleted
- Exhausted
- Lethargic
- Listless
- Sleepy
- Tired
- Weary
- Worn out

Pain

- Agony
- Anguished
- Bereaved
- Devastated
- Grief
- Heartbroken
- Hurt
- Lonely
- Miserable
- Regretful
- Remorseful

Sad

- Depressed

- Dejected
- Despair
- Despondent
- Disappointed
- Discouraged
- Disheartened
- Forlorn
- Gloomy
- Heavy hearted
- Hopeless
- Melancholy
- Unhappy
- Wretched

Tense

- Anxious
- Cranky
- Distressed
- Distraught
- Edgy
- Fidgety
- Frazzled
- Irritable
- Jittery
- Nervous
- Overwhelmed
- Restless
- Stressed out

Vulnerable

- Fragile

- Guarded
- Helpless
- Insecure
- Leery
- Reserved
- Sensitive
- Shaky

Yearning
- Envious
- Jealous
- Longing
- Nostalgic
- Pining
- Wistful

All of these feeling states are in service to us as *messengers* of whether or not we are getting our needs met. To get a more holistic perspective on what is going on behind you or your client's emotions, try picking one to three emotions from the feelings list, and then see what needs they correspond to below. For example, I am feeling *confused, frustrated* and *nervous* because my needs for *clarity, acceptance,* and *safety* are not yet met. Approaching feeling states with a curious perspective about what needs are emerging for truthful exploration can create empowerment for you, your HHB, and your clients. When you uplevel your Healing Gifts to include actively modeling any safe form of conscious communication, you can naturally increase authentic communication as well as diminish conscious and unconscious manipulation in all your relationships.

One note of caution here: if you were taught that expressing your emotions directly and having needs is inappropriate and selfish, you may be tempted to use any communication tool manipulatively at first. Practicing any communication modality with a commitment to truthful, shame-free, and respectful interaction will increasingly free you and your Healing Gifts from attracting drama and energy imbalances. Holistic Healers also sometimes try to be all things in support of all people. While it is absolutely true that the love you bring and the Source conduit that you are as a healer can always be helpful, adapting your communication as a form of persuasion will likely create a lot of confusion and resistance later. This kind of energetic bait and switch can be connected to arrogance and thinking you know how to 'fix' others.

Here's the Compassionate Communications list of common human needs, sorted into general categories:

Autonomy
- Choice
- Freedom
- Independence
- Space
- Spontaneity

Connection
- Acceptance
- Affection
- Appreciation
- Belonging
- Cooperation
- Communication
- Closeness
- Community
- Companionship
- Compassion
- Consideration
- Consistency
- Empathy
- Inclusion
- Intimacy
- Love
- Mutuality
- Nurturing
- Respect/self-respect
- Safety
- Security
- Stability
- Support
- To know and be known
- To see and be seen
- To understand and
- Be understood
- Trust

- Warmth

Honesty

- Authenticity
- Integrity
- Presence

Meaning

- Awareness
- Celebration of life
- Challenge
- Clarity
- Competence
- Consciousness
- Contribution
- Creativity
- Discovery
- Efficacy
- Effectiveness
- Growth
- Hope
- Learning
- Mourning
- Participation
- Purpose
- Self-expression

- Stimulation
- To matter
- Understanding

Peace

- Beauty
- Communion
- Ease
- Equality
- Harmony
- Inspiration
- Order

Physical Well-being

- Air
- Food
- Movement/exercise
- Rest/sleep
- Sexual expression
- Safety
- Shelter
- Touch
- Water

Play

- Joy
- Humor

Website: www.cnvc.org Email: cnvc@cnvc.org
Phone: +1.505-244-4041

Setting and Holding Sacred Space

One of my favorite communication tools that I have used and loved from the beginning of my career as a Holistic Healer was inspired by a very gifted woman, who I saw for intuitive sessions. I noticed that when she "set space" for our time together with a verbal preamble, my body relaxed and I thought to myself, "Whew, she's got this. I can just focus on my questions while she leads us." What a privilege to be trusted to do that for another person when they are likely sharing things with you that their pastors and parents might never hear.

The healing session preamble I use evolves occasionally, usually in alignment with what I am working on with my HHB. It always includes the elements of *protection, intention,* and *direction.* I evoke it out loud, silently or by touching my tongue to the roof of my mouth. This symbolically and literally connects my mental transmission to my Source receiving zone at the pineal and pituitary glands located behind the bridge of the nose. Glands are now understood scientifically to be the mechanical part of our bodies' manufacturing and distribution system for the chemical *messengers* (including hormones). I use this grounding and centering invocation before all sessions, most mediations, and occasionally when I get really wrapped around the axel about something to realign my energies:

Infinite Source Matrix within and around us
I honor, request and allow on behalf of All,

A healing intuitive alignment with
The Highest Good of All

I call forth from Source
A cleansing, clearing, healing and sealing of
All objects, experiences and artifacts herein

I command that all light beings present
work through Source Energies,
align the frequencies for the comfort of our physical
experiences
and move unconditional love
IN ALL WAYS
from now toward infinity.

A regular session preamble not only aligns and elevates healing frequencies, it creates communication continuity, safety, and trust for your clients who work with you over time. They come to trust that whatever drama is swirling in either of your lives, when they get on this preamble *elevator* with you, the doors will always open onto the same safe space they've cocreated with you before. Many practitioners I have worked with use preambles for their own space setting and holding reasons and to support communicating their own beliefs and values. A preamble can serve to create energetic ground rules, personal boundaries, and disclosure statements, giving the subconscious minds present the opportunity to harmonize. That foundational harmony can be a healing of its own. A preamble and/or a session closing statement can also be gracefully designed to contain clear messaging "updates" about your Healing Gifts and HHB as they evolve over time.

Developing Your Healthy HHB Boundaries

Another practical benefit of developing a session preamble or invocation is that it clearly communicates when you are engaging your healer mojo for someone else, versus having a casual conversation. Veronica, a life coach in Colorado, told me that when she started, she was working mostly with family and friends. When she decided to start offering her healing work professionally, she used her preamble as a gentle way to transition into being paid for that work.

If a friend or relative started to ask her professional advice about something, she would quietly wait until they finished talking and then asked them, "Should I set space for a session right now so we can look at that?" She found that it quickly and politely sifted out those who wanted to use her energy for free from those ready to invest in their growth process with her as a guide. It often helped her make a conscious choice about if and how to proceed. Was *she* ready to do a healing session, or was it more appropriate to schedule one for later and just enjoy the personal relating as a friend or relative in the moment?

It is very helpful in the healing arena to set and hold clear communication boundaries. Over time, you learn where flexibility helps or hinders your particular client/holistic guide style and relationships. Often, the bottom-line benefit to working on this is that your friends and family learn that they need to respectfully stay conscious of where your boundaries are, versus not even knowing that you have them.

Understanding and Emanating Your Inherent Value

Another big pivot available at this level of your HHB development process is the opportunity to gain ease in clearly communicating your worth. This pivot elevates your healing work to an increasingly relaxed transmission. Some healers like to begin integrating this uplevel with internal mantras while they are with clients, to keep themselves a clear conduit for direct client-to-Source connection. My favorite right now is "We are Happy, Healthy, and Whole." A healer friend from Australia says, "only love" repeatedly whenever she catches herself holding her breath in client healing sessions. Others do vision boards, books, and journals to stay connected to the inherent value they are aligning with and embodying by offering healing services. Somedays, our esteem and resulting vibrational set-point fluctuates as we skirt the more ragged edges of our growth curve. Consistently projecting the value you deeply desire your clients to have access to through your Gifts is one of the sacred mirrors they are often asking you to hold up for them. Having a list of healing peers that you can refer clients to when you sense that they would be better served elsewhere is a communication technique that lets your clients know that you have their best interests at heart and reflects your authenticity as a human being with natural limitations.

Cocreating Your Elevator-up Perfect Sales Pitch

Perhaps your past professional work has involved enough sales or marketing elements that you have attempted to create a "thirty second elevator pitch." Maybe this exercise made you as claustrophobic as the poor soul who was your captive audience. You have uncovered enough so far at previous levels of this process about your desires and the value of your healing services to create a short, perfect service message in this fifth level. Aim for it to be an information invitation that resonates with what your listener fortuitously found you to hear. Radiate how you feel about your Healing Gifts and stay aware of the tone of your voice. Try speaking it with soft lips and eye contact, remembering to say it with an open heart.

After someone asks you what you do, smile and communicate in fifteen words or less what you do, how you do it, and why. Then ask them what they do. If you feel a positive, uplifting connection, you can ask an inviting question that will help you understand what they heard or wanted to hear in your communication, and decide if you want to connect any further with them about your work. For example, I help holistic healers start their dream businesses to secure their work freedom. How about you, what do you do? For other inspiring, holistic examples, visit www.invitingbalance.com/reSources.

If you are busting a gut to tell someone what you do and they haven't asked you yet, you can ask them what they do and still get the same info about *if* and when you want to connect professionally with them, or even share information about your services. As you practice this energetic, verbal handshake, you will get a clearer sense about what your potential roles are in the dialogue, whether that's mostly listening or speaking.

Being new at *holistically* communicating your authentic message can be a very vulnerable experience if you are still working out your initial HHB desires, intentions, and the direction of your service. So, it is helpful to have a truthful connecting message that holds no risk for you to speak confidently until you feel more vulnerability is appropriate for all involved. Keep in mind that you may be connecting with someone who has either no idea or a negative idea about what they think you want or do as a healer. For example, one relationship counselor client I know named Ben who gets asked all the time, because he is male and dresses professionally, "What do you do?" He often responds firstly, "I help people decide if they want to improve their close relationships right now." Then, if he senses any resistance in himself or them, he will smile and say, "What's your work?" He feels this gives his receiver immediate control over how intimate they want to get in this first conversation. He believes this really communicates more than he could ever say about his value for respecting his client's privacy and comfort zones.

As you uplevel your HHB messaging and start practicing consciousness communication skills that reflect your authentic style as a Holistic Healer, your "organic" outreach will gain momentum as you are able to communicate with more ease and consistency about your HHB. Consider that people are more likely to do what they see than what you say. The simpler your messaging is, the easier it will be for you to model authentically across a wide variety of outreach opportunities.

Also, over two decades of working with all kinds of people in the Wellness Service Arena, I have learned that the simpler I able to communicate how I am going to help someone achieve the results they are asking for, the greater chance they will comply with our cocreated holistic healing options. *Compliance* is actually key to sustainable client results and the sustainability of you guiding them over the long haul.

This level's assignment for your HHB business plan includes some foundational work with the messages you can use for your direct outreach for new clients and longer-term marketing messages.

Level Five Holistic Healing Business Plan Outline Assignment

At Level Five, note or edit what you know so far about your:

- Main, first focus service of your HHB and its top ten benefits for your ideal client
- Holistic Healing Business Name—will people who don't know you easily know what you offer?
- Work Location/s—consider safety, ADA access, parking, and noise levels during your office hours.
- Hours of Operation—when are your ideal clients most available?
- Contact Information—How is your ideal client most easily going to connect and schedule with you? What level of privacy is important for your work-life balance and the safety of you and your relations?
- Description of your HHB (fifty words or less)—What is the main healing service you provide and problem it solves?
- Main goal of your service for self, clients, and other stake holders—What's your HHB *why*?

- Description of your three closest competitors: focusing on their who, what, when, where, why and how.

- Describe members of your current or future dream team for your HHB. Try imagining a group of two to ten healers that have more complimentary than perceived competitive services. What circle of providers would your ideal client most benefit from having aligned on one support team? For example, I was an Office Manager at Crossings Center for the Healing Traditions (http://crossingshealing.com) while I was in Massage Therapy school nearby. Their approach, which is still thriving twenty years later, is to offer each client a care team and healing options versus just acupuncture or holistic nutrition.

- Draft ten, fifteen and thirty-word messages about the benefits of your HHB for any of the following listeners: self, business partner, life partner, potential ideal client, existing client, investor, your spiritual mentor, your child (or close younger relation), their teacher, a stranger behind you in line, your parent, or another category of person that you interact with at least once a month. Hint: See if your HHB messages are simple and clear enough to be almost identical regardless of who you have the honor of transmitting them to and stay aware of any groups you feel awkward or defensive connecting with.

Chapter 9

LEVEL SIX—EXPANDING YOUR INTUITIVE SENSORY SKILLS TO DEVELOP ABUNDANCE WITH YOUR HOLISTIC HEALING BUSINESS

The mind can proceed only so far upon what it knows and can prove. There comes a point where the mind takes a leap-call it intuition or what you will-and comes out upon a higher plane of knowledge. All great discoveries have involved such a leap.

– Albert Einstein

Y ou were likely wondering in the months or years leading up to your Elevator–Up! Process, "What's next?' Maybe you started reading self-help books on life purpose or career change. You likely started feeling a divide between your past worktime preferences and the yearning to explore your own way in the world professionally *and* personally. Over the first five levels, your mind has been hard at work feeling and emoting, sorting, deciding, releasing, and embracing—*Whew!* Are we there yet?

Where you sit, breathing in and out in this moment, is the culmination of countless questions that your life experiences have sketched across your imagination for further contemplation, someday. Congratulations! That someday is *now*, and we are ascending to the sixth level of your Healing Gifts upleveling process. Here, you will remember and align with your advanced sensory skills to expand the abundance in and around your HHB. Some aspects may feel new and awkward initially, and others will simply be re-membered.

Warm Up:

I often see doubt and resistance as the two most common blocks to expanding abundance for my clients beginning their Holistic Healing Businesses. Here are two extremely simple tools I use with them and myself all the time to interrupt any chronic patterns around doubt and/or resistance. Practice them each once a day this week, using a specific doubt or resistance you have right now with your HHB.

1. *If you knew the answer, what would it be?*

When you notice yourself getting scared, overwhelmed, or receiving a lot of attention by complaining that you don't know what to do, be, or say, try this. Gently place your non-dominant hand over your closed eyes, eyebrows, and bridge of your nose.

Then, ask yourself, "If I knew the answer right now, what would it be?"

Prepare to have your mind blown out your ears when you experience what happens when you give your Inner Knower a voice and permission.

2. *One to ten emotional barometer:*

If you find yourself stuck for lack of clarity while choosing between two HHB options, ask someone to silently choose a number between one and ten. Then assign option one in your mind to numbers one through five and option two to six through ten. Ask them what the number was, and notice your immediate emotional response. If you feel positive, you have your answer. If you feel bad, you have your answer. If you feel neutral, ask a more specific question or trust that it doesn't matter which you choose and move forward with the easiest option. This barometer will entrain your brain to work more cooperatively and intuitively with your inner emotional intelligence.

Today Is Yesterday's "What's Next"

As we explore expanding abundance for your dream HHB from startup to sustainable, now is a good time to discern how your sensory tools can be enhanced to help you understand and integrate the direction you have been developing. It is the dance between your courageous imagination, and your evolving intuition that takes center stage here for your expanding HHB abundance. As a holistic healer, you are probably already more aware of the unseen support around your HHB and clients than those who are relating to healing from a symptom-relief perspective. You have been listening to your inner wisdom enough to at least be curious how the body-mind-spirit balance is such a powerful force for healing. My experiences with intuitive development training have allowed me to help thousands of people access everything they need for healing *from within*.

While there is no doubt that the amazing medical and technological advances of the last century have made it more possible to measure and diagnose what's happening within our bodies' mechanisms, ancient intuitive technologies still offer substantial empowerment for healers across the globe to address holistic health and healing. Logistical accessibility and affordability to 'modern medicine' unfortunately remains a mostly first-world luxury. How will your HHB holistically help resolve this profound, basic human need? By exploring and developing your inherent sensory capacities, you can add priceless value to what is possible for your clients' self-healing potential. This will naturally align you with more ideal clients and lead to more powerful referrals through their trust in your expanded sensory abilities.

Lots of healers develop their own bridging techniques, often based on modalities they have studied and personal healing experiences they have had or witnessed. Helen, a sound healer on O'ahu learned that combining basic yoga sequences scientifically proven to detoxify the body with gentle anti-microbial essential oils and vocal toning greatly enhanced healing results for her clients recovering from chemotherapy. If I can engage a client's curiosity about what is going on inside their body *underneath* their symptoms, their innate, homeostatic rebalancing system can often bypass their mental beliefs about how long it *should* take to heal an imbalance.

One great way to systematically calibrate with your unique inner compass and uplevel your Healing Gifts is to find an inspiring way to record what's happening intuitively as you work with clients. For example, if you keep conventional S.O.A.P. notes to track the Subjective, Objective, Assessment, and treatment Plan aspects of your client's healing sessions, you can engage your intuitive development by adding an "I" and keeping S.O.A.P.I. notes. The "I" for intuitive information tracks seen and unseen experiences you and the client have during and between your healing sessions. Here are some empowering "I" notes gathered throughout my twenty-year journey as a Certified Massage Therapist, Integrative Energy Therapist, Aromatherapist, Wellness Intuitive, and Certified Yoga Instructor:

'Client smells rosemary being diffused and reports a cool wave of energy starting at sacrum moving toward feet, and an overwhelming craving for pizza.' This note led to a few questions that connected her with forgotten memories of a grandfather that had molested her in his bakery as a child. She was able to eventually work with a referred hypnotherapist to forgive her grandfather, release her gluten intolerance, and finally have orgasms without a sense that she was doing something disgusting…. Tell me where you find that remedy in the pharmacy?'

'Client sees aqua and orange undulating energy behind his eyelids in the five-minute resting period after trigger point therapy behind the shoulder blades.' He begins the next session asking how he can get more colors to finish crying out his anger at himself for quitting Art School. He claims that he hasn't slept this well since he dropped out, but just now made the timing connection between his anger and insomnia. He estimates that he has spent eight years and over $6,000 in therapy, OTC, and on prescription drugs, seeking respite.'

'Client reports major positive shift in her anxiety after tuning in with the "From Survive to Thrive" topic in session six of her Intuitive Expansion Series'. She claims later that she was not previously aware that the attention she was getting from her mother by commiserating about finances was the only way they talked. She decided to ask her Mom about it and her Mom said she was relieved because she wanted to talk about something else moving forward. Her mom felt responsible to make sure my client didn't make the same money mistakes she made when she left her job to raise her thirty-five years before.'

By noting intuitive sensory perceptions like these and reflecting them back to clients, you empower them with a very valuable and safe space to take their healing session results *holistically* to another level.

Lastly, despite my learning and sharing over 22 different modalities as a 'healing elevator', I am always surprised at how most people have no idea (or permission) how to use their inherent intuitive Gifts. To address this in an empowering way for those who have resistance to taking responsibility for their own healing, I simply ask, "Does it make sense that the Organizing Intelligence behind all we can see and prove would give me intuitive capacities and *not provide in equal measure* to everyone else? Regardless of someone's beliefs, this inquiry aides me in understanding where to meet my client intuitively *and* appropriately.

Minding Your own HHB

Managing your Holistic Healing Genius and allowing others theirs is a very simple and effective way to accelerate abundance in your HHB. Abundance in all its forms *loves* cooperation. Whether your abundance goal is to secure your work freedom, financial independence, or to be held in community with copious opportunities to grow and share your knowledge (or all of these), refining your most effective and satisfying service keeps your mind, ego and efforts focused on *your* HHB. A pitfall that many budding healers fall into is trying to offer every service they can imagine to meet their clients' every need. Spiritual egotism can create unnecessary pressure within eager healers, implying that if they were *really* great healers, they would be able to solve any glitch a client presents. I *do* believe it's true that anyone can facilitate any healing when aligned with Source. And, I have had the road rash to prove that just because you can help someone doesn't mean you should.

One of the best benefits my healer friends and I continue to enjoy is the repeated reminder amongst us that there are plenty of people out there that can better help the clients that personally give you ice-cream headaches. We sometimes humbly mumble about how one of the responsibilities that accompanies the extreme privilege of being entrusted to facilitate a client's healing process, is loving them and yourself enough to tap out before the brain damage. My buddy Darla says that when she gets the strong urge to 'shake like a wet dog,' she gets out her contact list and gently hands her client some referrals she trusts to better serve the scenario.

Identifying and Clearing Your HHB Growth Blocks

Even though it can take practice to employ clearing tools that work for your particular blocks to abundance, the results of trying seem to have a very strong and clear return on the time, energy, and courage you invest. Reflect back on just the Warm-Up exercises you chose to practice while elevating your HHB with this upleveling process. What growth blocks are you now handling more powerfully because of this upleveling work? You probably know that new habits can take time (average of twenty-one days) to become progress paths. I bet you also *feel* at this level which 'blocks' are your best opportunities to substantially increase the abundance you attract through your HHB. That is your expanding intuitive sensory system calibrating with your HHB desires, goals, and Higher Purpose.

Some of the most common abundance growth blocks I see Holistic Healers transcend while expanding their sensory skills are:

- I don't feel right about making money/more money for my healing services.
- I am not sure how to get enough practice at this new holistic tool before I can integrously charge for it.
- I don't know anyone who will pay for this service right now.

- I need more time to figure out who my target audience is and what to say to them that sounds smart.
- What will my mom/ dad/ spouse/church/boss etc. think about me until I make more money at this than at my old job?
- My healings aren't that big of a deal to potentially turn my life upside down for…
- How will I ever find the right people to help me, or to partner with?
- I keep changing my mind and putting off just starting.
- I don't have a business plan.
- I don't know how to time my exit from my current work.

Developing your advanced sensory skills will be a lot easier when you have broken down some of these distractions that are likely ricocheting in your mind. Consider making a list of your *perceived* growth blocks. Focus on one growth challenge every thirty days to get deep, sustainable results, and increase your abundance. If you feel overwhelmed by what seems like a long list of obstacles to professional abundance, gift yourself ten minutes right now to jot them onto a piece of paper. Seal them in an envelope dated a month from now and give them to someone who will not let you open it until that date. This will give you some space from your inner critic while you focus on *one* growth block that month. This can also help you sidestep the temptation many healers with perfectionistic tendencies face: as a healer, I need to be perfecting every aspect of my life (especially how financially successful my healing business looks to others) in order to be a great healer. A lot of clients have shared with me that they feel intimidated by 'great' healers and that they feel more willing to invest themselves with someone they think can really relate to *their* challenges. Once again, empathy out-serves fame because it is something everyone wants, needs, and can embrace their own healing through. What if you acknowledge your limitations for their sacred service of building empathy within you and for your clients? Journal on which of these hold a charge or bring up other blocks for you with your HHB. If you want to go deeper with what you discover in this experiment, we can arrange some focus time to help you lift yourself out of particular blocks.

Meditation is one direct way to amplify your intuitive sensory skills and get really clear about what kind of chronic thought patterns may be hindering your abundance from expanding. If quieting your mind is unpleasant for you, you can begin with short movement mediations and build up the amount of time you spend on them as you begin to crave the endorphins released from things like going on a nature walk, swimming, or practicing five minutes of yoga. One of my yoga teachers says that to expand your consciousness, the most powerful meditation you can do is the one you will *consistently* show up for and start to crave. After the initial period of discomfort that many people feel when beginning a new meditation practice, it is common to enjoy a feeling of peace in your mental space. This is one of the easier ways to advance your sensory skills, which tend to emerge when and where you make space for them between your thoughts.

Whether you are more clairvoyant, clairaudient, clairambient, clairsentient, or claircognizant, you will find as you develop any one of these, the others will be enhanced. Therefore, it is important to be mindful of expanding them at a pace that honors your life situation and nervous system. Appropriately pacing sensory expansion is as important as the expansions themselves for the sustainable upleveling of your Healing Gifts.

As you work through the HHB business plan assignment for this level, you can get the best results by keeping your focus on how you will feel when you decide you are abundant. As you prepare to add to or update your business plan here, experiment with where you feel most grateful with your HHB process right now.

Level Six Holistic Healing Business Plan Outline Assignment

At Level six, note or edit what you know so far about your:

- Main, first focus service of your HHB and its top ten benefits for your ideal client
- Holistic Healing Business Name—will people who don't know you easily know what you offer?
- Work Location/s—consider safety, ADA access, parking, and noise levels during your office hours.
- Hours of Operation—when are your ideal clients most available?
- Contact Information—How is your ideal client most easily going to connect and schedule with you? What

level of privacy is important for your work-life balance and the safety of you and your relations?

- Description of your HHB (fifty words or less)—What is the main healing service you provide and problem it solves?

- Main goal of your service for self, clients, and other stake holders—What's your HHB *why*?

- Description of your three closest competitors: focus on their who, what, when, where, why and how

- Describe members of your current or future dream team for your HHB. Try imagining a group of two to ten healers that have more complimentary than perceived competitive services. What circle of providers would your ideal client most benefit from having aligned on one support team? For example, I was an Office Manager at Crossings Center for the Healing Traditions (http://crossingshealing.com) while I was in Massage Therapy school nearby. Their approach, which is still thriving twenty years later, is to offer each client a care team and healing options versus just acupuncture or holistic nutrition.

- Draft ten, fifteen and thirty-word messages about the benefits of your HHB for any of the following listeners: self, business partner, life partner, potential ideal client, existing client, investor, your spiritual mentor, your child (or close younger relation), their teacher, a stranger behind you in line, your parent, or another category of person that you interact with at least once a month. Hint: See if your HHB messages are simple and clear enough to be almost identical regardless of who you have the honor of transmitting it to, and stay aware of any groups you feel awkward or defensive connecting with.

- Start working with a financial income and expense tracking tool like a ledger book, excel spreadsheet, or the QuickBooks (https://sbconnect.intuit.com/smallbusiness/) or Intuit Mint app (www.mint.com) to capture what expenses your HHB startup will require in the first year. Also document how much income you want to generate annually above and beyond your total expenses. Get as detailed as you can about exactly how much income it's going to take to keep you feeling financially safe and professionally satisfied. For legal and ethical reasons, make a list of three business finance courses (many are low-cost or free online or with your local SBDC https://americassbdc.org/) you can take and three CPAs you can phone interview as potential business partners by the end of your first ninety days in business. The financial data needed for your HHB business plan will vary widely depending on why you are sharing it. Tracking this basic info about your HHB and making an effort to align financial skills and support will create a great foundation to build upon. For legal or other business questions, you can check out www.justanswer.com.

Chapter 10

LEVEL SEVEN—CREATING SUSTAINABLE VALUE TO ENSURE YOUR HOLISTIC HEALING BUSINESS LONGEVITY

"Where attention goes, energy flows; where intention goes, energy flows!"

– James Redfield

Now that you have transcended the first six levels of your HHB Elevator-Up! process, we will culminate at Level Seven by addressing some of the issues that will come up as you start to see the long-term, bigger picture for sharing your Healing Gifts through your successful HHB. With your HHB needs and wants clearer, your professional passions embraced and ignited, your direction and actions fueled, your healing community connections initiated, your messaging gaining authenticity and ease, and your sensory skills amplified for attracting abundance, you are now ready to start considering your HHB's sustainability and longevity.

As you look back on what you have uncovered in your previous levels about your *whys* for starting your dream HHB, you can now see how a clear *why* can keep you moving in the right direction when you are navigating all kinds of fun and challenging aspects of getting your HHB started. Here's a warm-up exercise to up-level your *why* to inform your HHB's long-term sustainable value and growth.

Warm Up: Remembering Your Sacred Why Exercise

- As your connection and commitment to your HHB has grown through this process, you are likely starting to think beyond your HHB beginnings to generate more of what is working. Let's celebrate your progress so far by noting your top emotional, physical, intellectual and spiritual HHB *whys* so that we can clarify your current *Sacred Why*. This is the *why* that is connects your upleveled Healing Gifts to your Higher Purpose.

- Let go of all that still remains to be decided and done for a moment and allow yourself to feel the satisfaction of what your intuitive inspirations are *right now*.

- Once you have noted a key phrase for each aspect, go back and choose the one or two keywords for each that best represents that aspect's *why*.

- Now, combine those four to eight keywords in the most inspiring order to reveal your *Sacred Why*. If it feels like something you want to cherish and share, you are in the right zone!

- Here's an example of key phrases for each aspect with the keyword italicized, then combined:
  - Emotional *why:* to feel *empowered* to share my Healing Gifts *joyfully*
  - Physical *why:* to maintain and model *holistic health*
  - Intellectual *why:* to *expand* and *exchange* holistic knowledge
  - Spiritual *why:* to live and serve in *alignment* with the Highest Good of All
  - *Sacred Why: expand exchange joyfully empowered holistic health alignment*
- Use this *Sacred Why* as a mantra for the next ninety days to remedy fear, doubt, scarcity, confusion, resistance, emotional numbness, paranoia, loneliness, negative self-talk, violent thoughts, stubbornness, stinginess, resentfulness, entitlement, spacing out, hiding from your HHB work, losing your train of thought, and anger aimed at authority/Source. For extra-strength dose, combine with a healing self-touch modality like lymphatic massage, EFT, Thymus Thump, Kundalini Yoga mudras, etc. You can use your *Sacred Why* like a mental GPS to help you redirect when you come up against HHB roadblocks.

Re-Membering My Healing Business Higher Purpose

All of the clarifying and releasing you've accomplished throughout the levels of this process can now yield another layer of satisfaction and value for you and your clients as you start to uncover and emanate the *Higher Purpose* of your dream-come-true Holistic Healing Business. If you are already working with the Law of Attraction, you are in touch with the aspect of Spiritual Law that claims you are responsible for *asking* for what you want, letting all the reSources around you magnetically *respond,* and then *allowing* what you are calling in to manifest. We look at this, your Spiritual Return on Investment, in this seventh level to help you know how to work with the fruits of your HHB process efforts.

It is said that "what is measured can be improved," so knowing how you measure your HHB progress is as important as knowing what you want to achieve, and which actions will yield best HHB results. Going back to some of your notes from the Satisfaction Surrender exercise at Level Two, you've likely refined exactly what it will take for *you* to feel like you are successfully living and aligning with your Higher Purpose through your HHB. Now is the time to review those notes, maybe repeat the exercise from your upleveled perspective, and quantify in writing what your measures of success will be for your HHB in ninety days, six months, and at one year from now. Try to include at least one success measure for your emotional, physical, intellectual, and spiritual aspects at each of these stages. If your HHB's main purpose is to ultimately enable another later venture, now is a good time to think about what factors will need to be handled to end or transition your HHB or to end it to make room for the next, better platform for your upleveled Healing Gifts. This can be very basic for now; it is just important for your new HHB to understand if you imagine it ultimately pivoting into something different. This is likely years down the road, but feel free to contact me at invitingbalance@ gmail.com if you have more questions or concerns about this aspect now.

Holistic Healer Tools for Maintaining a Positive Presence

One very rewarding benefit of being a professional Holistic Healer is that maintaining a healthy, balanced lifestyle greatly enhances your healing talents and HHB success while you are up-leveling your own self-care. You are modeling *thrive over survive* in a world that is laden with messages about quick fixes and pushing through your pain instead of listening to it. The healing that moves through you and your preferred modalities is clearing you and upleveling your Healing Gifts as it goes. As your own vibration elevates from simply being the conduit, you will likely gravitate toward simpler pleasures and experience deeper contentment with less effort.

Here are some examples. Enjoy visualizing gentle, cleansing energy in your shower water as a way to effortlessly clear negative psychic energy. Place a small picture or symbol that represents something you are grateful for because of your Elevator–Up! efforts in at least three places you find yourself feeling drained or frustrated. You could uplevel your bathroom mirror, car dash, keyboard, cellphone case, or cubicle into a positivity portal with this ten-minute time investment. The next time you order extra whip cream, use your enhanced sensory skills to experience the endorphins and dopamine rush without apology.

For an extra boost, surprise a friend who has been cheering you on with a treat, and enjoy the high together! Write three things in a small journal you keep at your bedside that you are grateful for each day. As you are gaining consciousness after a night's sleep or power nap, send someone in greater need than you love and appreciation up and over through Source. Offering Source-aligned healings can have an energy-freeing effect that is like the opposite of an addictive habit. As you use your gifts positively and proactively, you need progressively less energy to accomplish that same action *with better results*.

Another way to increase your business sustainability is by practicing going as slow as you can stand with your preferred healing methods in client sessions. This builds your spiritual endurance as you courageously allow your clients more permission and space to be extra messy (if needed) and liberated. This balances the energy exchange, as most of the work unfolds with you as a witness and accountability partner versus the heavy lifter and hazmat crew. If you have invested any love in nurturing a toddler, this is like the patience you develop by taking the time to let them practice autonomy while learning to walk within the safety of your uplifting stewardship versus carrying them around for your efficiency or control. If you have ever been trained professionally by a really integrous sales mentor, this is like the honor you received through a thorough *show, tell, try, do* process; they *showed* you what to do, they *told* you how they best do it, they *tried* it with you, and then they got they heck out of your way and let you *do* it yourself before you got too scared of your power to serve.

Owning and Communicating about
Your Source Connection

Getting clear and comfortable communicating your beliefs about the impact of Source Energies in your HHB is top-shelf transparency that will enhance your sustainable value and contribution in your healing sessions. Gently and unflinchingly standing witness to what you and Universal Assistance cocreate plants a seed within your clients' healing journeys. They, too, have the birthright of Source Connection that is never severed, just forgotten. A tool that a lot of my healer clients work with to help sustain their contribution and value is the Universal Assist List (UAL.) This came to me from Source when I was practicing for my Integrated Energy Therapy certificate and found myself mentally exhausted and physically thirsty after the training process.

When I asked my training mentor about this, she suggested the UAL tool because she noticed that people with highly developed intellects/egos seemed to feel deeply supported and renewed by working with one. Basically, you keep a private list of all the pressing things in your life that would benefit from having some Source Assistance, placing all new items at the top of the list and deleting resolved items weekly or as they are resolved. Pause before deleting each resolved item and notice what Universal support you accessed for the resolution. Aside from the practical benefits of staying organized with this basic list, you will start to notice that as you relax about the items as they move further down the list, the more easily you receive support in their resolution. This tool creates a fun and easy way to practice and track the *Ask, Allow, Receive* technology at the core of The Law of Attraction.

Some Holistic Healers also feel greatly supported and amplified by working with an ethereal council or team. Your sacred service alignments are usually very specific to where you are in your development as a healer and your spiritual beliefs about the appropriate role of the Unseen. I have seen holistic healers met at every imaginable juncture in their service by a loving presence that shows up however they are willing to recognize it. As long as these forces are materializing within the sacred space you set and with your client's permission, their identity matters less than the results your client receives. If you feel ready to invite the support of your Ethereal Council into your Holistic Healing service, here is a Reunion meditation that can help you get *reacquainted*:

- Fifteen minutes before a day of client sessions, visualize or sit in the space you will be offering your service.
- In your mind's eye, imagine who or what you would feel safe enlisting healing help from; maybe it's an Ascended Master you keep hearing about or any animal energies your client expresses a fondness for.
- Next, ask the being for what purpose are you reuniting right now and confirm intuitively that your connection is in Alignment of the Highest Good of All.
- Be open to the idea that the purpose of the pending session and intention for specific healing results may only be part of why Source is aligning energy through you today.

- Later, when you set space at the start of each session, recall the mental image of the potential helpers and invite them to support you and your client safely and gracefully.

Increasing Sustainable Energy Through Your Body

Utilizing your physical body to access ethereal connection and sustaining energy can also be very powerful for helping you sustain your HHB longevity. Whether you prefer breathwork, yoga, or other mindful movement modalities, finding and regularly using at least one body-based technique daily will greatly increase your HHB development stamina. Here is a yoga-based movement meditation with one posture for each of the seven levels in this process. You can use it to keep positive energy moving in your physical body. This promotes a positive magnetic vitality that builds emotional balance, mental strength, physical flexibility, and spiritual openness over time. Visit www. invitingbalance.com/reSources for other physical upleveling techniques and visuals on this yoga series.

- Level One—*Trust*—Forward Fold; bending forward at the waste with your knees slightly bent and letting the upper body dangle to encourage surrender. Enjoy three slow, deep breaths.
- Level Two—*Satisfaction*—Cat/Cow; alternate flexing your spine toward the sky and ground while on all fours to enjoy increasing energy and endorphin flow. Inhale while your spine is arched toward the floor and exhale while it is arched toward the sky.

- Level Three—*Direction*—Boat Pose; from a seated position on the floor, rise your feet parallel to the floor with knees bent and arms extended straight out from your shoulders, while using core muscles to balance on your sit bones to fortify willpower. Hold pose for three nostril breaths before relaxing to the earth for one minute.

- Level Four—*Connection*—Tree pose; Balance on one foot with your other foot in a comfortable position off the floor, with palms joined at your heart center to join the energies of earth and sky. Hold for three breaths.

- Level Five—*Ease*—Mountain pose; with your feet hip's width apart, gently lift and stack your body from toes through the crown of your head to enjoy the feeling of natural alignment. Enjoy three deep breaths.

- Level Six—*Abundance*—Bridge Pose; while lying faceup with your knees bent and heels near your tush, raise and lower the pelvis in sync with your breathing to release fear and resistance for ten deep breaths.

- Level Seven—*Contribution*—Child's Pose; sit gently back on your heals from a kneeling position and allow your upper body to fold toward the floor and relax into a grateful thought. Finish with three deep breaths through the mouth.

As you summit this apex level on your Elevator-Up! Process, it's time to draft the Summary section for your HHB business plan. This final segment creates the perfect opportunity for you to reflect on the contributions your HHB will make as your legacy project. This is the work that you will be most expanded by gifting to the world. It may be something you enjoy developing and nurturing for the rest of your life before you pass it on to the next generation of Holistic Healers.

Holistic Healing Business Plan Outline Assignment

At Level Seven, note or edit what you know so far about your:

- Main, first focus service of your HHB and its top ten benefits for your ideal client
- Holistic Healing Business Name—Will people who don't know you easily know what you offer?
- Work Location/s—Consider safety, ADA access, parking, and noise levels during your office hours.
- Hours of Operation—When are your ideal clients most available?
- Contact Information—How is your ideal client most easily going to connect and schedule with you? What level of privacy is important for your work-life balance and the safety of you and your relations?
- Description of your HHB (fifty words or less)—What is the main healing service you provide and problem it solves?
- Main goal of your service for self, clients, and other stake holders—What's your HHB *why*?
- Description of your three closest competitors—Focus on their who, what, when, where, why, and how.
- Describe members of your current or future dream team for your HHB. Try imagining a group of two to ten

healers that have more complimentary than perceived competitive services. What circle of providers would your ideal client most benefit from having aligned on one support team? For example, I was an office manager at Crossings Center for the Healing Traditions (http://crossingshealing.com) while I was in Massage Therapy school nearby. Their approach, which is still thriving twenty years later, is to offer each client a care team and healing options versus just acupuncture or holistic nutrition.

- Draft ten-, fifteen-, and thirty-word messages about the benefits of your HHB for any of the following listeners: self, business partner, life partner, potential ideal client, existing client, investor, your spiritual mentor, your child (or close younger relation), their teacher, a stranger behind you in line, your parent, or another category of person that you interact with at least once a month. Hint: see if your HHB messages are simple and clear enough to be almost identical regardless of who you have the honor of transmitting it to, and stay aware of any groups you feel awkward or defensive connecting with.

- Start working with a financial income and expense tracking tool, like a ledger book, excel spreadsheet, or the QuickBooks (https://sbconnect.intuit.com/smallbusiness/) or Intuit Mint app (www.mint.com), to capture what expenses your HHB startup will require in the first year. Also document how much income you want to generate annually above and beyond your total expenses. Get as detailed as you can about exactly how much income it's going to take to keep you feeling financially safe and professionally satisfied. For legal and ethical reasons, make a list of three business finance courses (many are low-cost or free online or with your local SBDC https://americassbdc.org/) you can take and three CPA's you can phone interview as potential business partners by the end of your first ninety days in business. The financial data needed for your HHB business plan will vary widely depending on why you are sharing into tracking this basic info about your HHB and making an effort to align financial skills and support will create a great foundation to build upon. For legal or other business questions, you can check out www.justanswer.com.

- Start to draft your HHB Summary section that overviews the content of your business plan for your main readers. It will be at the beginning of your plan and lets the reader know why you are sharing it with them and includes and outline of what it will detail. Each time you share your business plan, you can customize this section to reflect who you are sharing it with and why. This is sometimes referred to as an Executive Summary.

Chapter 11
HOLISTIC HEALING BUSINESS
LAUNCH PROCESS OPTIONS

What a clarifying and empowering journey you have transcended in your Elevator–Up! Holistic Healing business building process. You are now looking down from your customized success summit and can see and feel so much more possibility and alignment for your Healing Gifts through your new HHB. This chapter is designed to help you start organizing all that you have gathered from your desires, thoughts, decisions, and actions into a simple business launch process.

Warning: Allowing this to come together here and now may create so much inspiration and momentum, that you should brace yourself for some serious fun and satisfaction!

Warm-up: Up-leveling Your HHB Manifesto

Let's begin by revisiting your written HHB Manifesto about how you want to feel when you have launched your Holistic Healing Business. Before you revisit the exact manifesto you crafted at Level Three, take two minutes right now to quickly write down what you remember without looking back. Try to touch upon your emotional, physical, mental, and spiritual self-aspects like you did when you created your original manifesto.

Now, reference your original HHB Manifesto at the end of Level Three and compare your original with what you just wrote. Note your answers to these questions about your comparison:

- What did you notice that surprised you about the original versus second draft manifesto?
- What are your three strongest feelings now?
- What specifically about your statement really uplifts you now?
- What are you wanting to add, delete, or polish about it now?

Note: If you skipped this exercise at Level Three, go back and commit fifteen minutes to completing it now. Everyone integrates processes in their own way, so it's not an issue if you are just now crafting your Holistic Healing Business Manifesto. It is, however, essential at this juncture to write it down for your launch process.

As you review your answers above, explore your awareness of how important (or not) going through this process has been for your HHB start-up and your capacity to sustain it. Leverage the energy of this revised manifesto to organize your energy for your HHB Launch. Having a launch plan may be the single-most important start-up effort you can make toward ensuring that your business is among the one out of two that succeed versus fail. Keep in mind two contextual notes about this fairly black-and-white statistic:

Clearly setting your own terms for *what* determines that your launch was successful is a very personal and powerful boundary holder for your business, clients, and your energy expenditure. If you already know that setting and holding boundaries is a steep growth edge for you in your business right now, then this will be key to your sanity in the days leading up to and years after your launch. Think of this like a literal space shuttle launch. The choices you make here and discipline you exercise *will* determine your HHB's initial trajectory, orbit, and your shuttle-mate dynamics.

When most people think of a business launch, they are thinking of a specific calendar date where all of their supporters and stakeholders (and maybe even competition) will gather at your business site or at your Chamber of Commerce for a red ribbon cutting/luncheon and promotional announcement about what early adopters will gain in discounts or services. Your HHB has the advantage that all service-based businesses enjoy because of the emphasis is initially on healing services over tangible products. You can choose to set up a launch window over a longer period of time that allows you to adapt and adjust as your business emerges on your local scene.

While I have seen well-organized, year-long launches create sustainable success for some HHBs, the sweet spot seems to be creating a launch that spans seven to ninety days. Stretching your launch out too long will definitely diminish its impact and likely not hold your target audience's attention in a direct enough way to engage them as long-term clients. Alternatively, creating a well-timed soft launch keeps you accountable to your plan while giving you an integrous way to test your HHB's services, value-added products, and marketing messages.

A very easy way to launch your HHB is to create a *sustainable* offer that directly addresses the main need/problem of your most desired type of client. If you design a launch promotion that focuses primarily on making X amount of dollars by the end of the year or a certain number of repeat clients by next spring, you greatly limit your capacity to sell and deliver your services in a way that would satisfy you if you were the customer. Consider how different and doable it feels to create a promotional offer that says something like this in your own words:

- I see you and understand your problem as …
- Trust my expertise to resolve it effectively within a V of days.
- If you are ready to resolve it now, you can be among the first X number of people to get Y results for an HHB launch discount of Z dollars.

Plan Your Launch Who, Why, What, Where, and When

A very tangible and usually enjoyable aspect of planning your HHB launch is its logistics. This can be very satisfying because it helps you cross the bridge from wanting to launch your business to actually launching it. When you map out the who, what, when, where, why, and how for your HHB launch, you get to enjoy all the benefits of having a dress-rehearsal that allows you to feel safety and ease before, during, and after your formal launch/launch period.

For maximum simplicity and minimum expense, start your launch logistics planning by identifying *who* will most benefit from your launch and its coinciding promotion. This happens before all of your brainstorming, to-do lists, trips to the loan officer, or social media sharing about your great news that you are preparing to launch. Use the questions below to get a crystal-clear sense of *who* is your best first audience. Keep in mind that for most people, it is *not* the incredibly smart, caring, and opinionated members of their families or informal fan clubs (your like, share & subscribe gymnastics team.) Your best *who* is someone who is looking to hire *you* to facilitate their healing in a way that they currently believe they can't.

Yes, there will be a loving spoonful of people who will hire you even though they *already know* they can DIY your offering but simply must hire you as the tour guide for a variety of reasons. Maybe they are lonely or feel confused about their problem and need your Sacred Listening and healing experience to clear their blocks. Maybe their wife, mother, or BFF asked them to please call you as soon as possible. While you should invite all levels of manifesting in your HHB launch process, it is better to launch for a *who* that is really ready to share the cocreation of their healing process with *you*. As a healer with a new HHB, focusing on this *who* will teach you more about yourself and your Healing Gifts than any marketing analysis you can buy. Here are a few questions to bring your best launch *who* into focus:

1. What do you feel is your most powerful asset as a healer, and who is already shopping for it? For example, if you are a doula specializing in supporting new moms as they transition from maternity leave back to their career, who most needs that support, and where are/will they be looking for it?

2. When you close your eyes and imagine someone that would be easy to open your healer's heart to, who do you see in your mind's eye; what is their gender, age, ethnicity, nationality, spiritual orientation, and other distinguishing characteristics? Write down the most prominent characteristics so that your subconscious can start to help you recognize and align with your best first audience easily.

3. Who can you tell has a general life attitude that is equal to or better than your own? Keep in mind that like attracts like, and you will want to generate a great HHB launch with people who are already living their gratitude and commitment to healing. In my own HHB, these are the people who ten years later still work with me and have referred many like-minded, easy-to-help clients. Another way to recognize these people is that they are not looking for you to be perfect, just fully present and committed to their process.

Once you know your launch *who*, the work of detailing and implementing your launch *why, what, where,* and *when* with your launch team becomes remarkably simpler and more effective. Here's an example of how knowing your launch *who* creates ease for HHB launch planning:

Janie, a holistic nutrition coach, visualized her ideal client as a forty-year-old professional Hispanic woman named Miranda. She belongs to her town's biggest fitness facility where Janie happens to teach yoga twice a week. When she closes her eyes, she sees this woman hiding her perceived imperfections in black, high-end yoga clothes that she pays full price for to slim her mid-section. She tends to live on skinny triple-shot lattes, power bars, and orders extra salad dressing on the side. She feels frustrated making dinner for everyone else at home who will not eat anything healthy that she cooks. She works across town and spends many hours listening to fitness self-help audios while stuck in commuter traffic.

From this brief but fairly vivid imagining of her ideal launch *who*, Janie can ascertain that one great launch *why* is to help busy women like Miranda use smart nutrition to get back their figure, physical energy, and self-esteem. Janie may know that it's all really about the emotional work underneath the what to eat, when, and for what results, but that's not what Miranda is shopping for online for at 11:30 p.m. on her "What's New" Lululemon bookmark.

She can also figure from this that an attractive *what* to engage Miranda respectfully with is a thirty-day *Fitness Foods That Lift Your Lines and Your Mood* support package. She could launch her HHB with this consultation service package in the week between Christmas and New Year's, when Miranda is likely percolating her better health New Year's resolutions. Partnering with the gym on her launch *where* and *when*, she can use gym space after Miranda's typical workout time to do a few soft launches for opt-in clients from her classes and general gym traffic. (Keep in mind wellness facilities are always looking to add complimentary classes to support their members). As a gift for attending a thirty-minute Smart Nutrition Q&A hosted by Janie and sponsored by the gym, Janie can share the thirty-day companion audio series that she will be releasing for X dollars at her official HHB launch at the end of January when her ideal clients will most likely need support to sustain their healthier intentions.

Obviously, there are unlimited successful combinations of launch logistics. The point here is to get a clear picture of which combination will best connect you with the ideal clients who you were born to best serve, *first*. Then, have a logistical plan in place that will help you transcend a lot of your fears and the resulting launch procrastination and distractions.

While you are formulating your launch logistics this week and experiencing increasing clarity about your easiest path to your launch success, notice where you spend most of your time communicating. Are you more at ease connecting on social media, or do you prefer in-person connection when initiating conversations? Do you want to practice communicating your service benefits with people you already know or people you've never met? How has that shifted through this Elevator–Up! process?

Once you are clear on *your right answers* to these clarifying launch logistics questions, the path to creating a launch team will already be fairly clear. You will be attracting new partners, places, and client relationships through the heavenly pivot from *if* you will be launching your Holistic Healing Business to your knowing your definite launch *who, why, what, where,* and *when.* Visit www.invitingbalance.com/reSources for an HHB launch checklist to prime your inspiration pump!

Chapter 12
HOLISTIC HEALING BUSINESS OBSTACLES AND OPTIONS

Wealthy the spirit
That knows its own flight
Stealthy the hunter
Who slays her own fright
Blessed the traveler
Who journeys the length of the light
– Dan Fogelberg

While every healer may face different obstacles at different junctures in their Elevator–Up! journey, it is very possible to navigate, manage, and sometimes leverage potential challenges by staying aware of them. Most healers I have worked with reflect that the challenges/opportunities touched on here have proven less daunting than dealing with the feelings of being caught off-guard by them. Our goal here is not to wrestle every possible risk to the ground until it taps out. We simply want to see what comes up for you as we benefit from reviewing what has challenged other healers who have bravely gone before you.

So, let's take a proactive, guided tour through the Zoo of Potential Challenges I have seen many healers transcend while stepping into creating and leading their HHB's.

Emotional Obstacles and Options

The most commonly *known* emotional challenge I have seen healers face is fear of failure and the most common *unknown* emotional challenge is their fear of success. You can alleviate a lot of emotional distress and fatigue by figuring out your current relationship to these to fears *before* you launch your business. Here are some questions you can journal about or discuss with a trusted mentor or therapist. It seems like the answers are more impactful when you initially explore them in the privacy of your power. If you prefer to process this with another person, choose someone who has no attachment to your answers and notice if you are trying to convince them of anything in the process.

Fear of Failure

- What are my brain, ego, and/or negative onlookers trying to accomplish by focusing on what could go wrong? Remember to really listen to what's behind their fears if you want freedom from them.

- What is literally the worst thing that could happen to you, your family, your reputation, and/or your finances by moving forward with my HHB launch? Have you addressed any or all of these in the seven levels of preparation you just transcended? Which of these fears is most alive in you right now, and how can you progress toward its resolution as you launch?

- When was the last time you dared this courageously and how did it go? What successes and failures from that effort can you leverage now?

Fear of Success

- What self-sabotage patterns are cropping up now that you are nearing your HHB launch? How are your sleep, nutrition, exercise, and relaxation habits supporting your emotional stability right now?

- What attention or energy do you gain by staying stuck and complaining about it? Who or what are you afraid of losing when your HHB blossoms? Can you consider letting go now or proactively mitigate the potential loss by communicating your fears to those involved or in your journal?

- How do you feel about all these different kinds of success: financial, loosening the grip of addictions, increased self-esteem, emotional stability, clarity, satisfaction of desires, knowing and living your Higher Purpose? How about becoming capable of sharing your heart and Healing Gifts with others without attachment, getting heard, gaining safety with your truths, understanding and using your inner compass, being a spiritual leader and mentor, adding value past your personal gain, allowing Source to steer, etc.? What other kinds of success are most important for you to use as your measuring stick? Which one is the most important for you to have a handle on by this time next year?

Other emotional obstacles can include fear of abandonment, fear of the unknown, and fear of what people important to you will do, say, or think about your Healing Gifts and your hard left out of conformity into a less structured, Work Freedom lifestyle. Remember that you get to decide how much to change, and how fast. If you are creating too much change too fast, your emotions, your body, and your intuition will all start sending you signals. If any *one* of these aspects is piping up, you are likely on the right track for positive change, and it is just unresolved resistance that is dissipating.

If, on the other hand, *two or more* signals are registering, consider if the emotionally triggering situation is asking you to adjust your boundaries or develop additional healthy coping strategies. Because our emotions offer us information specific to our private growth edges, it can be most effective to honor or at least listen to repetitive feelings. If you have ever tried to accomplish anything with or near an emotional toddler, then you *know* it's much harder to get traction with anything else until that child feels supported, so support your inner child emotionally if you want to rebalance distracting chronic emotional patterns. One way to do this is to explore H.A.L.T. before suppressing or ignoring your emotions. Gently ask yourself if your being emotionally triggered by *h*unger, anger, *l*oneliness or *t*iredness.

Physical Obstacles and Options

All healers are subject to plain old gravity. Keeping in mind that the wisdom that comes with experience can greatly out serve brute force for both you and your clients, helping you cope physically with all the changes you are living through. One thing a lot of healers go through when there HHB creates a pattern interrupt in their reality is the infamous *healing crisis*. One of my mentors who guided me through my aromatherapy certification said that starting something new is like cleaning out a neglected closet. You find lots of things you have been missing, a few things you've been hiding, and you usually make some kind of mess before you can call it done.

If starting your HHB requires a substantial uptick in your physical activity, you can choose to plan for that by keeping a very simple sleep/rest, food, and energy level journal on your phone, computer, or notebook. There are numerous apps for this, and it is worth your time to find one you can use for accountability to your physical being. Be aware that trying to control your entire life with apps can be an avoidance maneuver that can hinder your self-awareness more than elevate it. I recommend settling on a meditation app first. I like Insight Timer because it took me nearly five years to crave and accomplish mediation five to seven times a week, and that evolved only when I found an app that made it easy to show up for the consistent practice of it.

Through my own HHB development process, I learned that I am much more balanced physically when I meditate regularly. I know other healers, like Damien who offers Reiki, that only meditate when they get a very specific signal to do so. When I asked some of them why they do it this way, some said that if they meditate regularly without the impulse, they tended to use it more as an escape mechanism than a mindfulness tool.

Developing awareness of what and how different things effect your physicality usually creates more rebalancing than working with any particular modality initially. I attribute this to the human body's scientifically proven proclivity for homeostasis (balance). Have you ever noticed how much better your body feels after a healing session when you are given the space to consciously connect with what your body is communicating first? There is an unspoken permission you give your provider and yourself to explore specific areas and find relief when you share information about what's up inside your skin. Checking in with your HHB client's physical state is a great way to build trust and connection and can help you stay aware of what your body wants, too.

Lastly, knowing that good (eustress) and bad (distress) stress often register the same physical impact can help you more effectively pace your changes to honor your body temple. Even when things are going really well, your body and nervous system need quality sleep and downtime to counterbalance the physical cortisol fire drill that accompanies both good and bad stress.

Mental Obstacles and Options

Mental obstacles can be a scaffolding of thoughts we construct to justify our feelings first to ourselves, then to others. Often, we believe we are protecting our existence and nervous systems with these mental circuit breakers. Depending upon your beliefs about the relationship between your brain, mind, and thoughts, mental obstacles can be approached in a way that creates a sense of mental alignment and ease versus resistance or confusion. If you believe that your brain is an organ that houses your mind and emanates your thoughts, then being a student of your chronic thoughts is a *very* effective way to heal mental challenges.

If you resonate more with the idea that your mind and brain are the same thing and your thoughts are mostly involuntary, you may find it more effective to get really aware of how your brain regularly reacts to a wide but standard variety of inputs. These are the two most common mental belief structures I see healers grappling with at their HHB beginnings. If you are willing to explore and embrace (or evolve) the way your personal beliefs impact your mental state, you will streamline your use of specific modalities and amplify their results because you will naturally learn to discern mentally what is you and what is Source moving through you during healings.

If you have every been privy to creating a distraction while someone else gets away with something covert, then you are familiar with how your brain reacts to most of the challenges starting your HHB can present. Gently try to keep in mind that your brain's most basic enduring success is to maintain your status quo and therefore your current reality's survival. So, even when you know logically and feel clearly that it's time for a good change in your work life, you can be unconsciously dealing with ancient hardware and obsolete software creating something similar to the error message *CPU busy* or *does not compute*. Know that the more you show up for your HHB process, the more security and clarity you will have with allowing your HHB dream to realize.

Spiritual Obstacles and Options

I tread lightly here because it is important to me as a Holistic Healer to respect however someone chooses to express their spirituality. Two things that are common spiritual obstacles for healers and their HHBs are spiritual egotism and spiritual shaming. Whenever we take comfort in what we believe is the *right* thing to believe, I feel we are stepping on the hose of healing energy that can potentially move through us. It has been my experience that Source or Infinite Intelligence is *always* more capable of cocreating healing with my clients than my spiritual egotism.

If you are focused on looking or feeling perfect before you can help anyone else, you are missing out on a lot of love that moves through you more freely when you can just quietly show up and focus on how to meet your client where they are. For example, many of my intuitive skills training clients were shamed by their spiritual influencers when they were young for using their extra-sensory perceptions. When they came to me for massage therapy, I stood as a witness they needed to allow themselves to dive into remembering and developing their intuitive Gifts. If you leave with one helpful message from this chapter about obstacles and options, let it be this Source message I always get, without exception, with everyone whom I have had the privilege to serve:

"The source of all pain is resistance."

Listening to your pain (resistance) will always move you forward on whatever level a perceived obstacle presents!

Chapter 13

CONGRATULATIONS! YOU'RE IN HOLISTIC HEALING BUSINESS

You have successfully and sustainably started your dream Holistic Healing Business and created an empowering exit from your job that leaves everyone involved better off than you found them. You have saved yourself years of HHB start-up trials and errors, tens of thousands of dollars in popular but often ineffective HHB start-up advice, time, money, and energy pitfalls. Your upleveling prep work ensures that your Healing Gifts are accessible and are going to align great results as you courageously grow your Healer's Heart. I know you are experiencing both a quiet pride and palpable relief from most of the inner conflict that used to block you from upleveling your Healing Gifts and starting your dream HHB. Maybe you started this journey mainly for your own purposes and then ultimately embraced your Higher Purpose for the benefit of the whole tribe of Homo*sapien*. Consider how your expanded capacity to simply *care for yourself* more sustainably supports humanity's evolution to Homo*spiritus*. Drafting your Holistic Healing Business Plan and launch process empowers your HHB sustainability and can help you navigate necessary adaptations while staying in alignment with your personal values.

Your Elevator–Up! process created a new understanding, acceptance, and inspiration with your inner compass that started your dream HHB the very first moment you started upleveling within this process. By transcending these seven levels and embracing your Healing Gifts, you have become the *Healing Elevator* for yourself and your HHB clients that you have been yearning to liberate. All the uncomfortable and awkward gaps in your confidence have been bridged or greatly narrowed. You've uncovered your deepest desires and gained new understanding and use of your own inner compass to amplify all manner of abundance for your dream HHB. All this upleveling has inspired your most authentic messages about your Healing Gifts to sustainably attract your ideal clients. As a spontaneous evolution of all this groundwork, you are now crystal clear about *how* to leave the stayed structure of your current work and start your HHB, and you're empowered to cocreate enduring value with Source for your clients and the countless people they love and care about.

Take a moment to ask yourself:

"Did I ever imagine I would experience and gain *so much* in this process"? Now, celebrate your initiation as the HHB Leader you are with gratitude for your courage and commitment by writing down your favorite aspect of each Level. You can create a celebratory piece that I call Inner Compass Art for your altar or healing space to sustain your HHB inspirations.

- Level One/Trust/Root Chakra (red)
- Level Two/Satisfaction/Sacral Chakra (orange)
- Level Three/Direction/Solar Plexus Chakra (yellow)
- Level Four/Connection/Heart Chakra (green)
- Level Five/Ease/Throat Chakra (aqua)
- Level Six/Abundance/Third Eye Chakra (indigo)
- Level Seven/Contribution/Crown Chakra (violet)

Having gained more clarity about your optimal business choices and their impact, you go forth with lots more wiggle and wag room to be curious first and then maybe a little afraid of your bigness, instead of living your life in fear of what you might be missing.

Through these seven levels, you have aligned with and allowed experienced, holistic help to support you and your HHB start-up. This sets an authentic, holistic precedent for your HHB clients that it is OK and empowering to ask for and allow help. You have explored the fun and challenges other healers enjoyed while resolving (with Source and many Sacred Service Agents) this problem for themselves and their clients repeatedly.

In eight weeks from exactly where you were, you lifted your Healing Gifts through these levels from a dream to a holistic, professional fresh start. You've found and focused your desires to ignite the inspiration that will sustain your HHB efforts for many years to come. You've taken effective actions from clear intentions to start your HHB successfully. Embracing a heart-centered community around your HHB members and their successes has created a whole new level of connection to your Higher Purpose and your life experience. Learning to effectively and authentically communicate has strengthened your Holistic Healing Business message and services. Developing your advanced sensory skills amplifies your flow of abundance through everything you and your HHB elevates. Your cocreation of self-sustaining value ensures your Holistic Healing Business growth and is now the source of substantial contribution in all your communities.

Thank you for our time, your trust, and this Elevator–Up! cocreation.

I wrote this book for *you* because I understand the healing power that clarity in your HHB choices, increased confidence in following your own intuition, and inspiration to cocreate a healing community with other awake beings amplifies in all of us. While our daily, individual desires may be moving targets, holistic healing is a natural, self-sustaining force that I *know* together we can continually and joyfully expand our alignment with.

ACKNOWLEDGMENTS

Thank you to Angela Lauria and The Author Incubator's team, as well as to David Hancock and the Morgan James Publishing team for helping me bring this book to print.
And…

Many mahalos for all the support afforded me by Source through all these divine beings!
The Grace Space Ethereal Master Mind reSourcers
Ester and Jerry Hicks/Abraham
Beth and Hugh Furman
Mary Anne and Paul Lenker
Suzanne and Joe Kobayashi & Irene Lacey Nepute
My Beloved Raymond; Alisia, Crista, Dillon, Travis &
Ava, Melissa, Phil, Carol, Chuck& Sarah Meek
Della & John Donaldson
The Hoffman Quadrinity Process team
My Sanctuary of LUBOF family
The Goddess Holly Burger
The Inviting Balance Tribe; Dana, Mitzi, Bear, Gini, Meredith,
Emma, Helen, Don, Carol, Tricia, Darla, Veronica, Ben, Shelly,
Pam, Isa Maria, Paula, Victor, Sarah and Janie
Melissa Wilson and Lynn Pizzitola
Paulo Kromerelli & Jeannie Pheasant
Yogi Bhajan, Kundalini Research Institute and the Soul of Yoga
Brother Sandeep Goel
Brian Tremblay
The Karen Family
Mrs. Kennedy
Gamma Phi Beta Sisterhood
Dr. William Hanna

THANKS FOR READING GIFT

Thank you for your courage to uplevel your Healing Gifts for the Highest Good of All! I know this book gives you a great start at fulfilling your HHB dream. As a thank you for reading this book, please schedule a free thirty-minute Holistic Entrepreneur business consult with me at www.invitingbalance.com/freeconsult so I can hear more about how your dream HHB is evolving.

If you want more customized help getting your HHB started ASAP, apply for a spot in this book's eight-week Elevator–Up! Companion program by visiting **www.invitingbalance.com/elevatorup**.

Let's stay connected:

Linked In: www.linkedin.com/in/grace-danielle-meek-cmt-cyt-iet-5a5144b1

Facebook: www.facebook.com/GraceDanielleMeek

Instagram: www.instagram.com/invitingbalance/

Twitter: @InvitingBalance

ABOUT THE AUTHOR

- Twenty years of experience serving clients in the Holistic Wellness Arena
- Certified Hatha & Kundalini Yoga Instructor, 2013-2014
- Wellness Intuitive, 2006
- Integrated Energy Therapist, 2004
- Certified Aromatherapist, 2002
- Certified Massage Therapist, 2001–HI #15193
- B.S., Family & Community Development/Dance, U of MD, 1992

Grace Danielle Meek's purpose as a Speaker & Author and Wellness Guide is to help you remember and develop who you are and why you are here in the most easeful, fun, and effective ways. After leaving the Washington DC area and corporate success in 1999, Grace's spiritual reSourcing path connected her with extraordinary teachers and friends through Colorado, California, and New Mexico before settling on The Garden Isle, where she is fortunate to lead Inviting Balance Wellness Services.

If you are here now, Grace has likely been where you are: searching for connection, balance, and meaning on your Journey. She shares her heart home on the Hawai'ian Island of Kaua'i with her soulmate Raymond, cocreating sustainability adventures and providing her clients around the world with intuitive direction and training to cocreate their holistic life balance.

CPSIA information can be obtained
at www.ICGtesting.com
Printed in the USA
JSHW011409111120
9509JS00001B/29